Race in a Post-Obama America

The Church Responds

DAVID MAXWELL, EDITOR

Contributors

Mary Gene Boteler
Laura M. Cheifetz
David Esterline
Jennifer Harvey
David Maxwell
Otis Moss III
Debra J. Mumford
Jessica Vazquez Torres
DeBorah Gilbert White
Frank Yamada

WESTMINSTER
JOHN KNOX PRESS
LOUISVILLE · KENTUCKY

First edition
Published by Westminster John Knox Press
Louisville, Kentucky

16 17 18 19 20 21 22 23 24 25—10 9 8 7 6 5 4 3 2

Scripture quotations from the New Revised Standard Version of the Bible are copyright © 1989 by the Division of Christian Education of the National Council of the Churches of Christ in the U.S.A. and are used by permission.

Book design by Drew Stevens
Cover design by Allison Taylor
Cover photo taken by The All-Nite Images

Library of Congress Cataloging-in-Publication Data

Names: Maxwell, David, 1960- editor.
Title: Race in a post-Obama America : the church responds / David Maxwell, editor ; contributors, Mary Gene Boteler, Laura Cheifetz, David Esterline, DeBorah Gilbert White, Jennifer Harvey, David Maxwell, Otis Moss, III, Debra J. Mumford, Jessica Vazquez Torres, Frank Yamada.
Description: Louisville, KY : Westminster John Knox Press, 2016.
Identifiers: LCCN 2015050539 (print) | LCCN 2016005044 (ebook) | ISBN 9780664262174 (alk. paper) | ISBN 9781611646665 ()
Subjects: LCSH: United States--Race relations--History. | Racism--United States--History. | Racism--Religious aspects--Christianity. | Race relations--Religious aspects--Christianity.
Classification: LCC E185.615 .R21257 2016 (print) | LCC E185.615 (ebook) | DDC 305.800973--dc23
LC record available at http://lccn.loc.gov/2015050539

Most Westminster John Knox Press books are available at special quantity discounts when purchased in bulk by corporations, organizations, and special-interest groups. For more information, please e-mail SpecialSales@wjkbooks.com.

CONTENTS

⸺ ⌾⌾ ⸺

FOREWORD

"How do I live free in this black body?"
—Ta-Nehisi Coates, from *Between the World and Me*

Many pundits hailed the election of Barack Obama as president as the end of all things constructed and construed by race. Over and over I heard men and women who live in gated and cul-de-sac communities trumpet a tale I failed to see. *Postracial* was the term that carried on the airwaves and in the Twitterverse: America had finally realized its noble creed of equality under the law and under God.

Yet as I listened I shook my head, wondering, What universe do they occupy? I listened to these words from the Southside of Chicago, where hope and tragedy dance daily for all children who are kissed by nature's sun. The promise of America has not cast its shadow or gazed upon the children who still hold the scars of forced exile and importation to this nation. I do not deny the triumphs, the moments of celebration and progress in our imperfect yet sturdy democracy. But this socially constructed ideology called race remains the original sin of our nation. Our institutions carry the residue and scent of race.

America doesn't see this.

To Ta-Nehisi Coates, impassioned chronicler of the open secret that America struggles to acknowledge, racialized thought and imagined supremacy are the myth and doctrine undergirding our democracy.

As he argues in his book *Between the World and Me*, the nation takes race as a defined and unchangeable reality, like a "feature of the natural world," and therefore feels absolved from doing much about it. He writes,

> Racism — the need to ascribe bone-deep features to people and then humiliate, reduce, and destroy them — inevitably follows from this inalterable condition. In this way, racism is rendered as the innocent daughter of Mother Nature, and one is left to deplore the Middle Passage or the Trail of Tears the way one deplores an earthquake, a tornado, or any other phenomenon that can be cast as beyond the handiwork of men.[1]

In this climate, our common explanations for the persistent disparities that are found in education, criminal justice, housing, and wealth fall into two camps. One argument looks at racial disparities through the lens of poverty, economic policy, and wealth creation and comes to the conclusion that these factors doom the poor, especially poor people of color. The other argument is made through the lens of cultural deficiency, claiming that people of color need to be injected with the wider Protestant work ethic and values of responsibility to close the sociological and material gap.

Sadly, both camps fail to confront the unspoken American belief that Coates names in his writing: being black and human is considered an oxymoron in much of society.

Blackness is viewed as a deficiency to be expelled from one's psyche or reformed in order to be palatable to the majority culture. More than a century ago, W. E. B. Du Bois spoke of this duality of the African soul that must try to heal in the face of a forced sociological schizophrenia, that "sense of always looking at one's self through the eyes of others, of measuring one's soul by the tape of a world that looks on in amused contempt and pity."[2]

Racism is not expunged by the elimination of blackness. Racism is not exorcised from the American lexicon through a doctrine of moral deficiency. It is eradicated by Christians only when we reject these myths and come to grips with the beauty of Africanness and dare to live out a new Christianity that is not beholden to European views. We fight these myths by admitting they exist. We fight them by facing the biblical mandate about what the Lord requires: to act justly and to love mercy and to walk with deep humility before God.

As you read through the pages of this book, my prayer is that each chapter will challenge, disturb, and ultimately inspire. America is in need of antiracism activists, preachers, and thinkers who are not people of color. America desires voices with a moral center that dare speak truth to power and walk humbly with our God. These yet-to-be United States wait patiently for your voice, song, poem, essay, sermon, and action to join the cadre of women and men who seek to dismantle and repent from this original sin called racism.

The Rev. Otis Moss III

PREFACE

Cries of "Don't shoot!" and "I can't breathe!" reminded our nation that despite the jubilation over the election of the first black president, racism is living and breathing in the United States. Once again the country has been reminded of its original sin of racism.

A person of color was finally in the White House, which was rightly celebrated. However, President Barack Obama was not elected on an antiracism platform. In fact, while some great things have happened during his presidency in terms of racial justice, his administration deported more undocumented immigrants than any president in history.

This book began to be constructed in Chicago during a conversation with a diverse group of faculty and staff from McCormick Theological Seminary and local pastors in the fall of 2008, before the election of President Obama. The group identified a number of topics dealing with racism that churches might discuss. Those initial studies were published online at *The Thoughtful Christian* and were very popular. We have taken some of those studies, updated them, and added four new chapters taking into account the rapidly changing landscape of race relations in the United States. Despite the large and diverse group of impressive authors of this book, you will find a common approach and direction. We suggest that you read the entire book; however, feel free to jump to any chapter you like. The book may be read alone, but we hope you will read it with a group of people who want to discuss racial justice and to take action.

Many Christians taking part in the current discussion and protests across the United States do not want to sweep the original sin of racism back under the white carpet of complacency once the protests die down. We hope that this book will provoke lively discussion and urge a long-term commitment to confess and repair in order to one day be reconciled to one another.

INTRODUCTION

On August 9, 2014, my ministry came full circle in the death of Michael Brown.

I was raised in Mississippi, a young girl during the first civil rights movement. When Dr. King walked from Memphis to Jackson down highway 51 to complete the march started by James Meredith, he walked through our place, alongside our cotton fields. When our schools were desegregated, I saw children beaten—and I didn't nearly see the worst of it. Southern pastors who preached too much about "the situation" were asked to leave. Sympathetic, protesting Northerners who were asked to leave got in their cars and left. Southerners first had to go by the house and collect their family and belongings.

One Southerner who was asked to leave his pulpit in Starkville, Mississippi, was Bob Walkup. Years later, as a young minister, I sat in his living room in Auburn, Alabama, and heard him tell his riveting story. When he came to the end, I responded, "Oh, Bob, I don't know what I would do if I were ever asked to leave a church." He looked at me with kind eyes and said in his gravely voice, "Mary Gene, there are a lot of churches, but you only have one soul. Don't lose it." His words have been a constant source of encouragement to me in my ministry—and I have repeated them hundreds of times.

In some ways, my involvement in the situation around Michael Brown's death was a working out of the demons that plagued me from those earlier experiences. In fact, I have come to believe that God placed me in St. Louis at this particular moment in history, gave me time to develop deep relationships that allowed me to preach God's unrelenting word when the events unfolded in Ferguson. And let's be clear: Ferguson is just a code word for the systemic racism embedded in our institutions and the white privilege that is so ubiquitous that the privileged hardly notice it.

Michael Brown was a young high school graduate who was heading to college. He was raised by his mom, who did everything right. She worked at a well-known St. Louis grocery store chain, along with one of our church's bright graduate students. Michael had a father and a stepfather who loved him. He was no saint, but if the right to live was reserved for saints alone, every pew in America would be empty. As a pastor, I am privy to the white children who struggle with drugs, shoplift in the local stores—and have all their youthful indiscretions buried by sharp lawyers. Michael was not unlike many of the children the church has confirmed and patiently loved into adulthood—only he didn't have the protection that comes with whiteness.

Michael was a black man in a world that does not value black lives. There was nothing unique about the death of an unarmed black teenager at the hands of an overzealous police officer. It happens all the time. What made his situation untenable for the community was the fact that he lay on the ground for over three hours. His mother could not hold him. There was no real attempt to save his life. He lay on the street in front of the community—including children to whom he was like a big brother—and he died.

The reaction of the community was immediate. White clergy sensed that we had to take our cue from the black community. "What do you want us to do?" we asked. One of the problems is that clergy had not previously built relationships that would allow us to respond quickly in such a volatile environment. That left us in the difficult position of building those relationships while responding to this tragedy. It was messy, and the news media took every advantage of that messiness.

The traditional leaders in the black community just assumed that they, by default, would direct the response. But quickly it became clear that there was, forming from the grass roots, a group of young leaders who didn't require approval or wait for the direction of their elders or the church. In fact, they viewed the complacency of the older leaders, preachers, and politicians as a mitigating factor in the death of so many young black men. For too long, they felt the church had suggested that the victims were responsible for their own victimization—pull up your pants, change your diction, and engage in the politics of respectability. What is being called the second civil rights movement is solely the responsibility of these young, brilliant leaders whose desire for freedom absolutely trumps their fear.

The first four months were extremely challenging. Every night there were meetings. Every night there were protests. A small group of clergy from various traditions was trying to follow the live streaming and be present when needed. Generally there was a call for support every night. It was exhausting. We had scores of people coming from out of town for the big events, and they all needed hospitality. Many organizations were trying to provide leadership, and no one was clear about the lane in which they needed to travel. There were those looking to serve, and there were those looking for fifteen minutes of fame. Again, it was messy. Out of that came some remarkable coalitions that continue to meet weekly; one involves sixty or more organizations working together to change the system.

We slept little. On the streets until midnight, we were up and in the office or hospital in the morning. One night while protesting in Ferguson, the group was called to Shaw, another area where another young black teenager had been killed. When we arrived, the police tape was still up and the investigators were doing their work. Someone pulled me aside to meet the boy's mother. She could only cry and say, "What did I do wrong?" I went to the morgue at 2 a.m. with his father. They would only let him see his son's face, and he left wondering, "Why won't they let me see his body? How are they planning to manipulate the evidence?" I have seen too much not to be skeptical. I have come to understand that trust in the system is another benefit of our whiteness.

I was fortunate to serve a congregation that understood my place to be both in the pulpit and in the street—or, at least, a large majority did.[1] At times it was a balancing act. I had one elder resign from session and the church on Facebook. We exchanged some emails, and by the next morning he wrote, "I would like to stay, if you will have me." I welcomed him with open arms, of course.

The turning point in the movement was the night of the nonindictment. We had known for months that Officer Darren Wilson would not be held accountable. For four months, churches and community groups had been planning for the day. We attempted to work with government and law enforcement officials to develop a plan that would allow people to express their pain, allow the protestors to exercise their First Amendments rights, keep the community safe—and, most of all, value people above property. I have nothing but the harshest criticism for Robert P. McCulloch, the prosecutor, who had no desire to work with the community and, instead, developed a plan that would ensure the worst possible outcome.

On the evening of November 24, 2014, after the non-indictment, our church gathered at 6 p.m. for worship. Following the service, my daughter and I traveled to Ferguson. Even though the crowd knew what was coming, we were holding on to a small ray of hope that justice would be served. When the decision was announced at 9 p.m., it was as if the very life had been sucked from people. There was wailing and crying and the breaking of glass. But then the familiar drumming started and the chanting began—and it was peaceful and cohesive. Suddenly, in the distance, we saw tear gas floating through the air, heading in our direction. We heard gunshots. My daughter and I held hands and tried to run away from the tear gas; we were not entirely successful. As we ran, we stopped to care for some of the people who were the most severely affected. With the help of a stranger, who turned out to be a clergywoman I had not previously met, we headed for our car but were trapped by a police car that was in flames. It had suspiciously been left unattended on the street.

After that night the protests continued, but many of us began moving away from the nightly gatherings and concentrating our work on faith-based organizing. The continuing protests are important, and I have nothing but admiration for those who see that as their role. A wonderful group of interfaith clergywomen began to study together and work for change. We had a number of women's marches. We called ourselves the Wailing Women, after Rachel: "weeping for her children; she refused to be consoled because they are no more" (Matt. 2:18). At one of these marches, I stood near a woman with a picture of her son at various stages in his life, from childhood to graduation. His name was Jeremy. I turned to her and said, "Tell me about Jeremy." And the tears began to pour down her face as she spoke, in great pain, of her beloved son. It was heartbreaking. The community has been filled with opportunities for sacred conversation. And change is coming. . . . one *resignation* (the word the establishment uses for "firing") of an official following another. We simply cannot let the movement stall this time.

For eight months, protestors chanted, "The whole damn system is guilty as hell," in a community in which most of the citizens thought the protestors were wrong. But the Department of Justice report is vindication, if not satisfaction. It clearly points out that crimes were committed, blacks were targeted, lies were told, and that the system is broken beyond a simple mending. What it does not do is hold anyone accountable. And that creates further pain and distrust.

Finally, Ferguson is every community. It is not the worst—not by a long shot. In fact, one could stand in Ferguson and spit in any direction and hit a municipality that is every bit as corrupt and racist. Every state, every city, every community. When we think that our community is different, we "deceive ourselves, and the truth is not in us" (1 John 1:8) There is not a person in the United States who does not live in Ferguson. Our response as people of faith is to decide what our baptism calls us to do about it.

This book is for Christians—especially white Christians living in the United States—to read, discuss with others, and initiate or continue a plan of action to confront racism. Some chapters are informative and offer reflection. Others suggest an array of actions you and your faith community might take. I urge you to take the time to read this book, to pray, to consider what plans of action you might take, to discuss with others, and then to start or continue confronting racism in your church, community, and nation.

The Rev. Mary Gene Boteler

PART I

RACISM DEFINED
AND RECOUNTED

CHAPTER 1

DEFINING TERMS

Much has been accomplished through civil rights legislation that has paved the way legally for racial equality. Nevertheless, racist attitudes and practices still exist. On the one hand, the election of the first African American president and the first Latina appointment to the Supreme Court offer hope for continued progress toward the elimination of racism. On the other hand, the Supreme Court's actions invalidating key parts of the Voting Rights Act, the continued instances of police killings of innocent people of color, and the burning of black churches and Muslim places of worship remind us that racism is still very alive and flourishing in the United States.

This chapter attempts to help define racism and some of the pertinent concepts involved in discussing it. The hope is that by the end of the chapter readers will have a deeper understanding about racism and the roles people can play to ensure its demise. Many of the terms and concepts introduced here are discussed more deeply throughout the book.

Defining Key Terms

Four terms that are often confused in discussions of racism are *culture, ethnicity, race,* and *nationality.* It is helpful to distinguish them.

Culture includes nonbiological characteristics of a group based on shared behaviors, thoughts, and values that are learned. Cultures often have symbols that identify them. Examples of shared culture might include hippie culture, Western culture, Middle Eastern culture, Latin culture, LGBT culture, Dallas Cowboy football culture, or racist culture.

Ethnicity also refers to social traits, not physical traits, that are shared by a human group. These traits might include a shared history, language, religion, culture, traditions, nationality, or tribe. People identify with one another as coming from common ancestors and sharing distinctive cultural traits. As opposed to race, people identify their own ethnic connection rather than it being defined and imposed by others. Some examples of ethnic groups include Native American tribes and Jews. Unfortunately, due to racism in the United States, many national, tribal, and linguistic ethnic groups have been lumped together into one single ethnic category, such as Negro, Indian, Latino, or white, which has created confusion between ethnicity and race.

Race refers to real or imagined physical traits that distinguish one group of people from another. It was first introduced in the United States as a biological concept to categorize humans based on skin color, hair texture, and eye color in order to privilege one group and to control other groups. (More on whiteness will be discussed in chapter 10.)

Nationality refers simply to one's country of citizenship. It is not an indicator of a person's race. A common mistake is to ask people their nationality when what is sought is their ethnicity.

Due to this country's history of categorizing people according to skin color so that light-skinned people could have privilege, much confusion exists between how to define oneself on government forms and other documents that request information about one's identity. The racial categories most commonly used today on most applications are white, African American or black, Hispanic/Latino, American Indian or Alaska Native, Asian, Native Hawaiian or Pacific Islander, and some other race or origin.

These categories and the high proportion of those who check "other," such as Arabs, demonstrate the development of racial identification over time, which will continue to change. Throughout the nation's history, those called white have been dominant and normative.

In 1790, as the United States began to shape its identity away from a colony and toward a nation, the first United States Congress began the process of legally codifying race with the passing of the 1790 Naturalization Act. This act limited U.S. citizenship to "free white persons of good and moral character." Not all people who were considered "white" today were seen as "white" in this period, either by legal definition or common understanding, but the passing of the 1790 act ensured that access to citizenship in the developing United States was limited to those whose ancestry was European.

Difficulty of Defining Racism

Racism is multifaceted and has both racial and cultural considerations. The complexities of racism make it nearly impossible to define as a singular concept. Although racism is informed by perceptions, attitudes, feelings, and behaviors associated with one's own racial group and other racial groups, the key factors that make racism what it is are the elements of power and privilege.

Part of the difficulty is the tendency to interchangeably define racism as *prejudice* and *discrimination*. There are differences between each of these.

Racial prejudice involves judgments, opinions, attitudes, or feelings formed before the facts are known or in disregard of the facts that contradict them related to race. We all prejudge others. Most all persons have prejudice against some other group. As long as we do not act on this prejudice to harm the other group, it is simply prejudice. Example: The belief that all members of another racial group are lazy, lack positive moral values, and are stupid.

Racial discrimination is the act or practice of giving different treatment to persons according to their membership in a racial or ethnic group. Example: A member of one racial group treats poorly or denies service to members of another racial group in a restaurant. Prejudice and discrimination are distinguishable and describe different realities based on race with varied consequences. Most often, and for the purposes of this book, when we speak of racism we are referring to the practice of racial discrimination in which those from the dominant race are harming people from other races. The following definitions are helpful in providing a foundational understanding of racism and how racism works:

> Racism is a system of advantage or privilege based on race.
> Racism is racial prejudice plus institutional power.

In the United States and some other countries around the world, the dominant racial group is white. In the context of racism, the system of advantage or privilege primarily benefits white people. Of course, privileges and advantages do not look the same for every individual white person, due to the multiplicity of identities each person carries.

Racism in its broadest sense has particular expressions in other countries around the world. UNESCO (United Nations Educational, Scientific, and Cultural Organization) has organized a series of conferences to address issues of racism around the world. Many countries have distinct experiences of discrimination in terms of race, often negatively impacting indigenous groups, certain ethnic groups, the caste system, or immigrant groups. Because racism is a social construct, each country experiences it differently. In this book, the focus is on racism in the United States.

Racism

intentional and unintentional
The personnel committee's policy is to interview members of various racial groups to meet the organization's diversity employment requirements. They continually select members of one racial group for the final candidate pool.

A teacher provides a reading list of contemporary authors to the class. The list features primarily white authors.

overt and covert
Members of specific racial groups are steered by a real estate agent to look only at housing in particular neighborhoods. Other clients are offered broader options.

A congregation's outsourced operating functions are always provided by individuals or businesses owned by members of one racial group.

connected to privilege
Some members of a college's student activities committee challenge the nomination for committee president of someone from a different racial group, stating, "We've never had a [blank] in that position, and now may not be the time."

A security guard routinely interrogates members of certain racial/ethnic groups while allowing others to simply pass by.

connected to power
Members of particular racial/ethnic groups are stopped while driving when they have broken no laws.

A health facility's expansion plans result in the displacement of community residents who are mostly members of one racial and economic group.

The Family of "isms"

Racism gets expressed in different ways, from patterns of access to schools, housing, employment, and health care; to language and assumptions about competency and ability; to hate crimes and violence. Racism should be "conceived as a family of *isms* based on race, or racisms."[1] Following are definitions of several types of racism and examples of each.

Individual/personal racism is an individual's belief in the superiority of her or his own racial group over other racial groups that is expressed through attitudes and behaviors that maintain those superior and inferior positions.

— A parent explains to a child that a classmate can't be as smart as she is because people in that racial group just aren't as smart as people in their own racial group.
— A worker expresses to a colleague that the new executive was hired only to meet a racial quota.
— A store manager instructs a salesperson to "keep an eye on" patrons who belong to particular racial groups.

Institutional racism includes laws, traditions, and practices that systematically result in inequalities based on racial preconceptions. It is the perpetuation of a double standard of treatment and opportunities evolving from a positive valuation of the dominant racial group (which in the United States is the group we refer to as "white") and a negative valuation of nondominant racial group members. Institutional racism may also be referred to as *systemic racism* or *structural racism*.

— A bank refuses mortgage loans for the purchase of homes in neighborhoods where mostly Latino/a, African American, and new immigrant groups reside.

— Local media coverage of an inner-city neighborhood is only about criminal activity.
— A congregation displays in its bulletins and information boards only images and cultural perspectives that reflect the dominant racial group.

Cultural racism combines elements of individual and institutional racism that express superiority or domination of one race's cultural heritage over that of another race. It is natural to have pride in one's heritage and traditions, but cultural racism comes into play when the dominant racial group holds power to define cultural values and the individual forms those values take, rewarding those who possess them and punishing or ignoring those who do not.[2] In the United States the dominant culture is white, and white people as well as people of color participate in enforcing the primacy of white culture.

— An Asian American parent prefers that her child be exposed to European classical musical forms instead of traditional Korean music in the child's diverse school.
— An African American receptionist at a medical office is noticeably agitated when communicating with patients who do not speak English.
— A school or professional sports team continues to use a Native American image as its mascot after community members have requested that it not do so.

Internalized racism involves the destructive patterns of feelings and behaviors experienced by recipients of racism when they adopt racial stereotypes, racial prejudices, and misinformation about their own racial group.[3]

— An Asian girl chooses the white Barbie doll because "she's the prettiest."

— Despite being the brightest student in class, a Latino boy chooses to sit in the back of the class and always defers to his white classmates.

— An African American worker, talking with other African American workers, insists that white people are natural leaders because they are smarter.

Environmental racism is demonstrated in the placement of toxic and hazardous waste sites, landfills, and polluting industries in African American, Asian, Latino/a, Native American, migrant worker, and working poor communities.

— A community's housing values decrease when it is discovered that the homes have been built on a toxic landfill.

— Children are experiencing symptoms of asthma and lead poisoning. A chemical plant is located in their community.

— State and city officials do not apply environmental laws, regulations, and practices uniformly across all communities.

Damages of Racism

Many who have been the targets of racism can readily express the harm of racism in their lives. What is often missed is the effect of racism on the individuals and members of groups who perpetuate it. Racism for many is defined on a personal level only. They view it as something that resides in attitudes and beliefs about one's own group's superiority and the complementary attitudes and beliefs that other groups are inferior. Some believe we simply need to concentrate on changing individual feelings, thoughts, and behaviors to eliminate racism:

To end racism, policies must change, racist behavior must stop, the injustices from racism must be redressed, and all people must recover from the damage done to them by racism. . . . To fully eliminate racism, we must heal three forms of damage[:] . . . damage done to individuals targeted by racism[,] . . . damage to members of targeted groups from "internalized" racism . . . [and] the corruption of the minds and spirits of those conditioned by society to act as the agents of racism.[4]

Individual transformation is indeed essential. However, we must not lose sight of how racism is built into the systems that individuals live and work in.

Steps to Challenge Racism

While learning and exploring the many aspects and dimensions of racism, one might feel overwhelmed that there is so much to learn and understand. Living within a society where racism exists, we have all been affected in some way. This includes experiencing feelings of hurt, pain, anger, guilt, embarrassment, shame, or powerlessness. As Christians, we are called each day to realize God's desire for us to be in community and, through Christ's example, are encouraged to move ahead boldly. There are many concrete steps we can take. Here are just a few:

— Be open to talking about the history of your racial group and other racial groups.
— Check to see if your assumptions are based on racial stereotypes or racial prejudices.
— Be open to continuous learning to address the harm of racism.

— Recognize the privilege and power you may have based on racial group membership.

— Understand the impact your cultural values may have on others in your work and worship settings.

— Be aware of your racial prejudices and stereotypes about others.

— Appreciate the challenges and opportunities presented by perspectives from diverse racial and ethnic groups.

— Create opportunities at church, at work, and in your community to be racially diverse and inclusive.

As people of faith, we view racism as an affront to God. Racism contradicts the belief that each of us is created in the image of God, and at its basic level, racism infers that some are more valued than others in the human family.

CHAPTER 2

THE BIBLE AND RACISM

Does the Bible support or oppose racism? In United States history, this question has been answered both "yes" and "no." White-supremacist groups such as the Ku Klux Klan have used biblical texts as weapons to promote hatred against racial minority groups. On the other hand, some Christian traditions have used the Bible's message of liberation as a resource for the promotion of civil rights and freedom for all peoples. In fact, biblical themes were central to the message of the civil rights movements in the 1960s. Thus, the Bible has played a role in both promoting and dismantling racism. It has been a proof text for groups seeking to reinforce white privilege, and it has been a rich resource of empowerment for communities struggling for liberation.

This chapter addresses issues of racism in the Bible, or the extent to which race is a factor within the biblical texts themselves. It explores themes that exist within the Hebrew Bible and the New Testament and includes a discussion of the cultural perspectives assumed within the biblical world.

Racism = Race Prejudice + Power

Race is the designation of a group of peoples based on an inherited set of phenotypical or physically identifiable traits (for example, skin color). Modern understandings of this concept emerged during the Enlightenment, coinciding with Western imperialism. As European empires expanded, they sought to classify the peoples that they encountered. Hence, the idea of race is deeply rooted in colonialism. By definition, racism occurs when a particular group exerts its sense of superiority over others on account of racial difference. Therefore, racism is defined not merely as prejudice—when one race is intolerant of another—but is also related intrinsically to power, that is, the ability of a group to exercise its sense of racial dominance over others.

There are two points of discontinuity with this definition of racism and the biblical world. First, the modern notion of racism is intimately connected to developments within the last few centuries in the West, though race as a concept certainly existed earlier. Modern U.S. racism would have been an unfamiliar concept to the biblical authors. Second, ancient Israel, because of its small size and lack of power in the ancient Near East, could not have enforced its sense of superiority over other groups in a way that would resemble contemporary racism. Ancient Israel was always a small vassal state caught in the struggles of large empires such as Egypt, Assyria, Babylon, and Persia. Like all social groups, the Israelites had beliefs that reflected their own culturally limited and even ethnocentric worldview. They exhibited prejudice against other nations, but they were fairly powerless to exert their sense of group superiority in an empirewide fashion.

Early Christianity also was a minority religion during its formation in the early centuries of the Common Era. It was not until Christianity found broader acceptance within the Roman Empire that the Bible became a significant source for shaping sociocultural norms in the West. Within the context of empire, biblical themes of group superiority, which were originally generated by historically particular and geographically specific minority groups, begin to take on a more ominous tone. The language of a divinely chosen people, for example, looks much different when situated within the context of a small, colonized state or religious sect than when this belief constitutes the ideology of an empire that intends to subjugate other nations because God is on its side.

Ethnic and National Identity in the Biblical World

Within the Bible, cultural difference is not identified primarily through physical traits. The more-dominant categories were ethnicity and/or religious difference. Ethnicity is tied to a group's common cultural understanding based primarily in national origin. Ethnic groups tend to have shared understandings of the world and history. Factors such as social customs and cultural norms inform these perspectives. When biblical scholars talk about the emergence of Israel in the hill country of Canaan during the late second millennium B.C.E., they tend to focus on issues related to the rise of a small nation that emerged originally from a confederation of tribes. National identity certainly played a role in ancient Israel's self-understanding, even though the term *nation* does not correspond precisely with the contemporary notion of nation-states, which is a product of historical developments in Europe during the eighteenth century.

The table of nations in Genesis 10 and the list of Canaanite groups in Deuteronomy 7:1 point to an awareness of other nations and peoples. In the prophetic materials, the Lord's judgment is proclaimed not only on Judah and Israel but also upon the surrounding nations (Jer. 46–51 and Amos 1:1–2:3). On the surface level, the biblical texts differentiate sharply between Israelites and these foreign "others," especially those who dwell in the land of Canaan. However, biblical scholars and archaeologists have determined that the ancient Israelites were virtually indistinguishable from Canaanites. Data from archaeological artifacts and material culture support this. Moreover, biblical scholars have shown that the traditions within the Hebrew Bible have parallels with religious and mythological texts from the region. In fact, according to one theory of Israel's emergence, the Israelites were originally a loose confederation of tribes who were made up primarily of disenfranchised Canaanites. Therefore, the sharp cultural differentiation between Israelites and Canaanites in the biblical material is a social construction.

Within the Bible itself, Israel is portrayed as a culturally distinct people who are set apart from the other nations (in Hebrew, *goyim*). They were not to worship like these peoples, nor were they to make treaties or intermarry with them (Deut. 7:2–3). This language suggests that the primary way the biblical authors understood social difference was through religious beliefs and an assumed set of cultural norms.

Historical realities following the Babylonian exile informed the ideas that we find in the Bible regarding Israel and its relationship to others. Most of the biblical traditions took shape or were substantially edited within the postexilic period (late sixth and fifth centuries B.C.E.). When the exiles returned after 538 B.C.E., their presence in the land was contested. These repatriating groups signaled their collective identity through sharp differentiation from the "people of the land." Hence, the biblical theme of Israel's cultural distinctiveness carries with it a particular meaning in this period. Postexilic realities also help to explain the strong tone found in the books of Ezra and Nehemiah against marriage with foreigners (Ezra 10 and Neh. 13:23–31). However, the books of Ruth and Jonah, which were also written at this time, provide a counterperspective to the xenophobic tones of Ezra-Nehemiah. Ruth is a Moabite who becomes the grandmother of King David; and the inhabitants of Nineveh, the capital of Assyria, repent and obey the Lord, unlike Jonah, the Israelite prophet. Even in these cases, however, it is clear that foreign peoples are not faithful on their own merits but are good insofar as they resemble faithful Israelites.

Within the New Testament, themes of a culturally distinct people persist. Even though the Gospel writers characterize Jesus as someone who disrupts existing social boundaries (Luke 5:30; 7:34) and challenges the religious status quo (Matt. 23:13–26; Mark 7:1–13), it is clear that the early Christians considered themselves to be uniquely situated in the world. Even in the case of Jesus, traditions exist that betray his sense of ethnic superiority. The account of the Syrophoenician (Mark 7:24–30), or Canaanite (Matt. 15:21–28), woman provides a poignant example. In this story, a woman comes to Jesus asking him to heal her daughter, who is tormented by an evil spirit. Jesus asserts that his mission is to Israel and that it would not be right for him to give the children's food to the "the dogs." His juxtaposition of the term *children* to characterize his own privileged group with the ethnic slur *dogs* to designate foreigners is a shocking example of the culturally specific character of Jesus' perspective.

Though Christianity sought to extend its vision of the world to include other peoples and nations (Acts 1:8), it is clear that a culturally specific lens provided the filter for its followers' worldview. Like other Jewish groups, the early Christians maintained their identity by dividing the world into two parts: God's elect and the other nations, also known as Gentiles. In the New Testament, the Greek word for these other peoples is *ethnē*, the plural of *ethnos*, from where we get the word *ethnicity*. Hence, both the Hebrew Bible and the New Testament have a worldview that assumes a culturally and religiously distinct core of people who differentiate themselves from "foreign" groups and who have a divinely chosen role to play in the world. These chosen peoples within the Bible emerge from particular social contexts. They are minorities within much larger societies or empires.

Themes of Racism in the Bible

Though the modern concept of racism does not exist in the Bible itself, certain ideas within it resonate with contemporary social dynamics. Some trajectories lend themselves to later interpretations that both seek to justify and to resist racism.

Biblical Themes That Can Encourage Racism

Chosen people/promised land. The books of Joshua and Judges depict in different ways the theme of a chosen people who are called to possess a promised land. This divinely sanctioned commission includes the extermination of the previous inhabitants (see also Exod. 23:27–33; Num. 33:51–56;

and Deut. 7:1–11). A key Hebrew word in this theme is *herem*, which connotes a holy thing or something dedicated to the Lord. In the case of the conquest narratives, *herem* includes the dedication of Israel's enemies and their possessions to complete destruction. This theme and its violent connotations are grounded in the central biblical idea of covenant; hence, they represent a critical way to understand God's relationship to God's people. A divinely sanctioned conquest lends itself to the possibility of racism in at least three ways: (1) the notion of a chosen people reinforces a group's sense of cultural superiority over others; (2) those who are not chosen are considered a threat to the purity of the "in" group; and (3) cultural difference is managed through the violent conquest of foreigners.

Separation from foreign others. The theme of separating from foreigners takes various forms in the Bible. It is especially prominent in the postexilic period, when groups of exiles sought to return to the land. When groups migrate, the need for clear social boundaries and identity markers becomes stronger. Within this context we find the impulse in the books of Ezra and Nehemiah to separate from foreigners, especially through the prohibition against intermarriage (Ezra 10 and Neh. 13). Foreign women are seen to be particularly threatening to the identity of the returning exilic community. Similar themes are present in the traditions about Solomon and his foreign wives (1 Kgs. 11:1–8).

The Lord's judgment on the nations. In the prophetic materials, God's judgment is often directed at the surrounding nations. Amos 1–2 uses the Lord's judgment of the nations as a rhetorical strategy to anticipate the message against Judah and Israel. Jeremiah 46–51 also contains a series of oracles against the nations. Theologically, God's wrath is intimately connected to the theme of justice. From the perspective of the biblical authors, the Lord's judgment against other nations provides a just resolution to problems in the world order. This theme universalizes the perspective of a particular group and subsumes the destiny of the world's peoples under Israel's God, who is seen as the sovereign of the earth.

Light/darkness. Another prominent theme within the biblical text relates to the symbolic idea of light overcoming darkness. In Genesis 1, God creates an ordered world out of chaos. The movement in this creation story proceeds from chaos to order, from darkness to light. This theme is also prominent in the New Testament, where it takes on connotations of enlightenment and characterizes the perspective of those who know God's salvation (John 3:19–21; Rom. 13:12; Eph. 5:8–14). This biblical metaphor, which also has strong connections with the seasons of Advent and Easter in the Christian liturgical year, implies that darkness is bad and light is good. Light overcomes darkness, and followers of the light are supposed to actively resist the darkness. In the United States, where race relations are constructed primarily within a black/white binary, this theme contributes to configurations of meaning that support the privileging of white over black, light over darkness.

Biblical Themes That Discourage Racism

Blessing to the nations. The Bible also contains themes that relativize or discourage racial or ethnic superiority. The promises to Abraham, for example, include not only the assurance of land and progeny but also the outcome that Abraham and his descendants will be a blessing to the nations (Gen. 12:3). Similarly, in the exilic period, Second Isaiah (Isaiah 40–55) proclaims that the once-conquered people of God will be a "light to the nations" (Isa. 42:6; 49:6). In this grand vision, the prophet declares that Israel's redemption will pave a way for all peoples so that the

Lord's "salvation may reach to the end of the earth" (49:6). Israel's primary role is one of a servant, whose task in the world is to be an example to the other nations.

The stranger in your midst. In the legal material of the Hebrew Bible, there is the strong charge to take care of the "stranger" (in Hebrew, *ger*) who lives in Israel (Deut. 10:17–19; Lev. 19:33–34). Moreover, the Israelites are to "love" this resident foreigner who is among them, for they themselves "were strangers in the land of Egypt" (Deut. 10:19). These passages not only encourage charity toward the *ger*, but they demand a sympathetic disposition, in which the ancient Israelites actually identify with the "other" who is among them.

Jesus' social boundary crossing. Though the Gospels depict Jesus in his cultural specificity, they also consistently characterize him as someone who challenges oppressive social structures. Jesus challenges the boundaries that serve to protect the privilege of the social elite. He encourages his followers to identify with the poor, he associates with the marginalized in society, and he challenges the ruling elite to practice justice. This aspect of Jesus' life and ministry has been influential for liberation and feminist theologians. The fight against social evils such as racism requires those who are willing to challenge existing boundaries of social convenience. Thus, Jesus serves as an example of how followers may align themselves with the oppressed of society, the marginalized whom God privileges.

There is no longer Jew or Greek. Finally, Paul's writings show an awareness of the culturally specific context of the Christian message, even as they seek to envision a new humanity that is more inclusive. In Galatians 3:28, Paul proclaims that in Christ, people are no longer "Jew or Greek." His words point toward a radical openness. However, immediately following this well-known verse, Paul goes on to say that this vision of humanity points to the inclusion of all peoples into the promises of Abraham (3:29). Hence, Paul's vision retains elements of his own specific Jewish worldview and theology. In practice, Paul asks his followers to keep their own ethnic particularity—Jews should remain Jews, and Gentiles should stay Gentiles. His manifesto in Galatians, however, points to a common shared identity in Christ. This Pauline theme has the potential to value the diversity that is represented in the human family while pointing to elements of unity that provide common ground for people of all races and ethnicities.

Conclusion

Christians are compelled to engage the troubled past between the Bible and racism while seeking to transform the world and others through an engagement of those same biblical texts. The Bible will continue to be used to support both justice and injustice, racism and liberation. This fact does not mean that we must do away with it or hold on to some pieces of the biblical witness and leave out others. This interpretative dilemma requires us to engage simultaneously the Bible, each other, and ourselves while holding faithfully to the complexity that comes from this engagement. Doing so will help us to live into the words of Micah 6:8: "He has told you, O mortal, what is good; and what does the LORD require of you but to do justice, and to love kindness, and to walk humbly with your God?"

CHAPTER 3

1492–1790: EUROPEAN COLONIALISM AND U.S. NATION BUILDING

All history is biased. The history we learn is written frequently from the perspective of those whose ways have determined the official story. The writers of history rarely limit their work to the presentation of facts. As historian Howard Zinn states, "The historian's distortion is more than technical, it is ideological; it is released into a world of contending interests, where any chosen emphasis supports (whether the historian means to or not) some kind of interest, whether economic or political or racial or national or sexual. Furthermore, this ideological interest is presented as if all readers of history had a common interest."[1] Rarely are our collective stories concerned with truth. History, Henry Kissinger argued, "is the memory of states."[2] Winston Churchill said, "History will be kind to me, for I intend to write it myself."[3]

The storytellers of the United States are no exception. Our national stories are a mix of symbolism and hero worship that seek to shape a strong citizenry instead of a

The Resistance: John Newton

Throughout these next four chapters, we will lift up names of some of those who resisted the dehumanizing practices we now call racism. In the period covered in this chapter, John Newton, author of the hymn "Amazing Grace," stands out. Newton served on a slave ship and eventually became a captain. Although he became a Christian, Newton's journey from slave ship to antislavery cleric was long. He wrote the words to "How Sweet the Name of Jesus Sounds" on the deck of his slave ship while waiting for the next cargo of enslaved Africans. Newton eventually renounced the slave trade and, after studying theology, became ordained in the Church of England. In 1788, he published *Thoughts Upon the Slave Trade* through which he denounced the morally corrupting effects of being engaged in such business: "I know of no method of getting money, not even that of robbing for it upon the highway, which has so direct a tendency to efface the moral sense, to rob the heart of every gentle and humane disposition, and to harden it, like steel, against all impressions of sensibility."*

*Quoted in Jonathan Aitken, *John Newton from Disgrace to Amazing Grace* (Wheaton, IL: Crossway Books, 2007), 320.

critically thinking one. Why do we tell the stories we tell? Why do we worship as heroes historical figures such as Christopher Columbus (that's the English translation of Cristóbal Colón), the Pilgrims, the frontier settlers, Woodrow Wilson, Andrew Jackson, and Thomas Jefferson? We too often oversimplify the complexity of history and ignore many ugly truths that are part of that history.

These chapters explore the historical development of racism in the United States. They engage in a "biased" exploration of history, not to oversimplify history but to bring its complexity to the surface. Our bias will be seen most clearly in our use of colonialism as the framework for understanding race and racism in the United States.[4] Why colonialism? Many studies approach the history of racism in the United States using African chattel slavery as the framework. We use an alternate framework that integrates the histories of African Americans, Native Americans, Latinos/as, Asian Americans, and other groups, focusing on the allocation and control of resources. Moreover, we draw from our experiences as people of color and from the wisdom of communities of color rather than the dominant cultural mythologies.

We are seeking to identify the patterns connecting the experiences of racial ethnic persons in the United States. After all, racism in the United States is more than just a black and white issue. The traditional dichotomous approach to understanding race obscures the fact that the United States has always been a nation of nations, diverse and complex. Robette Dias expands on this reality:

> These patterns are so deeply imbedded in our society, I can't look at our laws and systems without seeing them anymore. That they are so deeply imbedded but obscured in our collective psyche emphasizes the importance of understanding racism as White supremacy and looking at history through the lenses of colonialism and apartheid. We have been taught not to see these patterns, to see racism in disparate pieces as if it makes no sense. But seeing the three as interrelated and dependent strands, like the strands of a braid allows us to see the fullness of White supremacy in all of its manifestations.[5]

We are wrapped into our history—even if we do not mean to be.

European Colonialism Begins

"In year 1492, Columbus sailed the ocean blue . . ." and entered the narrative of a continent already populated by multiple civilizations. His voyage was part of the systematic empire building of Spain's Catholic monarchs, King Fernando and Queen Isabella, who after violently purging Spain of the Jews and Moors, were seeking gold and opportunities to spread their Roman Catholic religion. As a reward for returning to Spain with gold and spices, Cristóbal Colón was promised 10 percent of the profits, governorship over newfound lands, and the title of Admiral of the Ocean Sea.[6] With that agreement, Colón set out to find a new route to Asia, stumbling into a new continent along the way.

He was not the first European to land on the shores of the American continent. But unlike other instances of European contact, what followed his arrival was a bloody invasion of the lands where native peoples lived. Most commonly, we speak of the appropriation of land and the near decimation of native peoples portrayed as "discovery." For native peoples, what took place was conquest and genocide. In his report to the Spanish majesties, Colón wrote, "Thus the eternal God, our Lord, gives victory to those who follow His way over apparent impossibilities. . . . Let us in the name of the Holy Trinity go on sending all the slaves that can be sold."[7] This invasion greatly enriched participating countries at the expense of those already here: first Spain, then England and France, along with other European countries.

The Beginning of U.S. Nation Building

One hundred and fifteen years after the European invasion that began with Colón's arrival, the English established their first trading outpost on the Virginia coast in 1607.[8] As Sydney Ahlstrom explains, "The British knew, of course, that the terrain of the future United States was already inhabited. In fact, the conversion of heathen tribes would figure prominently among the stated objectives of imperial expansion in the New World, and long-lasting stereotypes of the Indians, as well as of the newly discovered Africans, were already taking shape."[9] The white colonialists and slave traders who were the dominant social group came to view Native Americans as vanishing savages and sought their dehumanization in order to justify genocide, to take possession of their land, and to exploit their land's resources.[10]

While on his voyage to the "New World," John Winthrop, future governor of the Massachusetts Bay Colony, wrote in 1630 of the desire held by the settlers that the new colony be like a "city on a hill" to inspire the world with the possibilities of a pure Christian commonwealth.[11] The incongruities between the settlers' Christian faith and their conquering ways were immediately apparent when John Winthrop declared the Indian lands where his colony was established a legal "vacuum" because the Indians had not "subdued" the land and therefore had only a "natural right" but not a "civil right" to it. Natural rights had no legal standing.[12] The conquest of the Americas broadly and North America specifically found the church morally compromised by its support and justification of an enterprise driven by the need of Europeans to possess, to control, and to acquire, even if the result was the systematic destruction of culture and peoples.

Enslaved Africans arrived in Jamestown in 1619, giving way to almost three centuries of dehumanizing practices that reduced Africans to property. What is unique about African chattel slavery is that these people were considered slaves for life, forced members of a large pool of free and cheap labor, and the vast profits bought through their continued enslavement were justified through a complex code built on pseudoscience and misinterpretation of Scripture that rendered the slaves as property. This strategy not only controlled the enslaved Africans but was also used to manipulate and control poor white people.[13]

Everything about the life situation of early Virginia settlers supported and justified their participation in the enslavement of people from Africa. The Virginians needed labor to grow corn for food and tobacco for export. Unable to enslave sufficient numbers of Native Americans, the enslaved Africans became the workforce of choice, since the Spanish and Portuguese slave trade had stamped Africans as slaves centuries earlier.[14] The enslavement of Africans is among the most disturbing enterprises undertaken in the formation of the nation we now know as the United States, and the church was not exempt from it.

In 1610, Brother Luis Brandaon responded in this way to concerns raised by a priest in the Americas about the enslavement of Africans:

> Your Reverence writes me that you would like to know whether the Negroes who are sent to your parts have been legally captured. To this I reply that I think your Reverence should have no scruples on this point, because this is a matter which has been questioned by the Board of Conscience in Lisbon, and all its members are learned and conscientious men. . . . Therefore we and the Fathers of Brazil buy these slaves for our service without any scruple.[15]

In 1706, the colonial government of New York declared that the baptism of a slave did not entitle said slave to freedom: "Be it Enacted by the Governr Council and Assembly and it is hereby Enacted by the authority of the same,

That the Baptizing of any Negro, Indian or Mulatto Slave shall not be any Cause or reason for the setting them or any of them at Liberty."[16]

African, Native, and European, black and white—all were misshapen equally by an industry that demanded human beings be fully dehumanized and turned into property. Not even baptism would provide freedom and self-determination. Moreover, in order to ensure that enslaved Africans and European-Americans related to each other according to their socially constituted roles, laws were enacted to keep them separate. In 1691, Virginia provided for the banishment of any "white man or woman being free who shall intermarry with a negro, mulatto, or any Indian man or woman bond or free."[17]

It is this history that runs through the veins of our national story. As the early Americans broke free from the yoke of European colonialism and began to shape the social experiment we now call the United States, the reality of Indian genocide and African chattel slavery also became a part of our country's history. Imbedded into our DNA were deeply held beliefs about the superiority of northern Europeans. After all, it was northern Europeans who "discovered" these lands. It was northern Europeans who brought "civilization" and "faith." This is most evident in the ways we have constructed the notions of citizenship. Who became a citizen of the emerging United States was determined by the newly established United States Congress in 1790 when it passed the first Naturalization Act in our history. This act limited citizenship to "free white persons of good and moral character," leaving out European indentured servants, enslaved Africans, Native Americans, and later freed slaves and Asians. Naturalization Acts in 1795 and 1798 only extended the period required to qualify for citizenship. Neither opened up citizenship to those who were not white.[18]

The 298 years that span the period 1492–1790 are most often described with words such as *discovery, expansion, nation building, formative, seminal,* and *growing.* These are the words many of us learned, but there are other words we need to claim: *genocide, slavery, land theft, conquest, systematic destruction of culture, dehumanization.* Those seeking to understand the roots of racism in the United States must expand historical frameworks to include these uncomfortable words, for these speak of the experience of people of color in this nation. These speak of the patterns of white power and privilege that limited the right to be naturalized as citizens to white persons until 1952.

CHAPTER 4

— ⊂⊙⊃ —

1790–1954: U.S. APARTHEID, COLONIALISM, AND NEOCOLONIALISM

This chapter focuses on just a few examples of U.S. apartheid, colonialism, and neocolonialism, beginning in 1790, when the Naturalization Act was passed, which determined who could be a naturalized citizen of the United States. The term *apartheid* arose in the country of South Africa to describe its policy of segregating and economically and politically oppressing the non-white population until recently. This term could easily be applied to describe the situation in the United States, where non-whites suffered forced migration and apartheid for most of their history. This period ended in 1954, when *Brown v. Board of Education of Topeka, Kansas* symbolized the beginning of the end of one form of U.S. apartheid as enforced by Jim Crow laws.

Citizenship

The U.S. government's first major legislation regarding immigration and citizenship in 1790 stated that only "free

The Resistance: Native Americans Protesting Forced Migration

Before they were forcibly resettled, the Seminoles said this to the U.S. government: "We are not willing to [say we will go]. If suddenly we tear our hearts from the homes around which they are twined, our heart-strings will snap"*

The Cherokee said this: "We wish to remain on the land of our fathers. We have a perfect and original right to remain without interruption or molestation. The treaties with us, and the laws of the United States made in pursuance of treaties, guarantee our residence and our privileges, and secure us against intruders. Our only request is, that these treaties may be fulfilled, and these laws executed. We entreat those to whom the foregoing paragraphs are addressed, to remember the great law of love: 'Do unto others as ye would that others would do to you.'"†

*Howard Zinn, ed., *The People Speak* (New York: HarperCollins, 2004), 10.

†Ibid., 9–10.

white persons" could be naturalized as citizens after a two-year residency and if it was determined that they were of "good character." This was finally amended in 1870 to include "persons of African nativity or African descent."[1] The long journey for persons of African descent who had been slaves was complicated by the Constitution's definition of slaves as three-fifths of a person. The three-fifths compromise between Southern and Northern states was part of Article 1 of the Constitution, which includes this statement:

Representatives and direct Taxes shall be apportioned among the several States which may be included within this Union, according to their respective Numbers, which shall be determined by adding to the whole Number of free Persons, including those bound to Service for a Term of Years, and excluding Indians not taxed, three fifths of all other Persons.

This compromise, between those who favored and those who objected to slavery, prohibited Southern states, where slaves were ineligible to vote, from fully counting slaves in their numbers. They could only count each slave as three-fifths of a person. This was an advantage to Northern states, which had more free white persons. Since states were required to pay taxes based on population, the South had to pay taxes on three-fifths of the enslaved population. This left out vast swaths of the population, such as Asians, who were neither free whites nor enslaved blacks, from 1790 until 1870.

This finally changed in 1870. The Fourteenth Amendment to the Constitution, ratified in July 1868, states, "All persons born or naturalized in the United States, and subject to the jurisdiction thereof, are citizens of the United States and of the State wherein they reside." However, even after the ratification of the Fourteenth Amendment and the passing of the 1870 Naturalization Act that included "persons of African nativity or African descent" as eligible for citizenship, other people of color were left in quite a bind. Many Asians approached naturalization by arguing that they were either "free white persons" or of "African descent." In 1922–1923, the Supreme Court heard cases from a Japanese immigrant and an Indian immigrant, both of whom argued they were "free white persons." Takao Ozawa, a Japanese citizen, wrote a brief outlining the ways in which he was American (his marriage, his disaffiliation with anything Japanese, his Christian faith) and also argued that his skin was white.

The Resistance: The Harlem Renaissance

In 1920s Harlem, a political movement was afoot. Black migration brought together artists who created a cultural movement of writing, music, poetry, painting, and other artistic media that dared to define itself, rather than let the dominant society define it. Included in this creative and liberatory movement were many artists and writers who were bisexual, gay, and lesbian.[*] Alain Locke wrote, "Harlem . . . promises at least to be–a race capital. . . . Negro life is not only founding new centers, but finding a new soul."[†]

[*]Richard Bruce Nugent, "Smoke, Lilies and Jade," in *The African-American Experience: Black History and Culture through Speeches, Letters, Editorials, Poems, Songs, and Stories*, ed. Kai Wright (New York: Black Dog & Leventhal Publishers, 2009), 451.

[†]Alain Leroy Locke, "The New Negro," in Wright, *The African-American Experience*, 453.

The Supreme Court ruled against him, citing that "Caucasian" and "white" were the same and that since Ozawa was not Caucasian, he could not be white.[2] Deciding to use this ruling of "Caucasian" as a qualifying factor, Bhagat Singh Thind referred to the science of the day. Social scientists placed Asian Indians within the Caucasoid region and also stated they were Aryan. Despite the Supreme Court's ruling of a few months before, the Court decided to ignore its own equation of Caucasian and white and held that "the words 'free white person' are words of common speech, to be interpreted in accordance with the understanding of the common man."[3] The decision went on to say that Thind could not be considered white according to the understanding of what was the common man.

Forced Migration and Apartheid
in the United States

People prefer to move due to factors within our control. We move to be near family or for a new job. We move so that our children can go to better schools or be exposed to a more diverse population. However, throughout U.S. history, many people of color and poor people have been forced to move. Apartheid is frequently a dimension of forced migration, as it keeps people legally separated from one another. In the United States, it has been based on race.

From Jim Crow to Brown v. Board of Education

Apartheid has taken two major forms in this period of U.S. history. The first is Jim Crow. Jim Crow laws were put into place throughout the colonial era and increased in the North after most slavery there was abolished. These laws were firmly established in the South after Reconstruction.[4] Jim Crow segregation was accepted in the North, and in the South it was clearly labeled, thanks to "whites only" signs posted over separate entrances, drinking fountains, and restrooms. Segregation continued in the North after World War II through the practice of restrictive covenants, agreements put in place by homeowners pledging never to sell their property to certain people (typically Jews and non-white racial groups).

The Supreme Court decision *Plessy v. Ferguson* in 1896 established the legality of "separate but equal" places of transportation, and thereby educational and other social institutions. This left Jim Crow in place, under the obviously false premise that resources were distributed equally between white and black segments of the population. While this set the groundwork for black colleges and universities to thrive, inequities between the two groups continued to deepen. The Supreme Court decision *Brown v. Board* of *Education of Topeka, Kansas* in 1954 struck down *Plessy v. Ferguson,* establishing that separate is not equal. A key piece of evidence was a study done observing the impact of segregation on the self-image of black girls. They were presented with a white doll and a black doll and asked which was pretty, which was good, and which was bad. The black girls chose the white doll as the pretty and good doll and the black doll as the bad doll. *Brown v. Board of Education* ended an era of legal segregation by race and laid the groundwork for the slow work of integrating a firmly segregated population.

Indian Reservations

The second form of apartheid in the United States during the period 1790–1954 is Indian reservations. Andrew Jackson, already experienced as a military man in killing thousands of southern Native Americans by the time he was elected president in 1829, said in his first message to Congress, "I suggest the propriety of setting apart an ample district west of the Mississippi . . . to be guaranteed to the Indian tribes, as long as they shall occupy it."[5] This sounds generous, but it was a promise broken, and the decision was made without the consent of the people being moved. The dividing line for the district was moved further west from the Mississippi because this law was not put into place before white settlers moved into Iowa and Wisconsin.

The Cherokee were supposed to be moved slowly over time, but when gold was discovered in Appalachia in 1838, five tribes, including the Cherokee, were rounded up and placed into camps, and then moved along the Trail of Tears, where 25 percent of the Cherokee died. Other Indians, particularly northern tribes, were also moved against their will to the territory of the Plains Indians. Many tribes who were placed on reservations were not consulted about

The Resistance: John Brown

In 1854, the decision over whether Kansas would be proslavery was left to majority rule. Proslavery activists attacked the profree town of Lawrence in 1856. John Brown, a radical white abolitionist, led a retaliatory attack against proslavery Pottawatomie, along with other acts for freedom. After being sentenced to death, he stated, "Now, if it is deemed necessary that I should forfeit my life for the furtherance of the ends of justice, and mingle my blood further with the blood of my children and with the blood of millions in this slave country whose rights are disregarded by wicked, cruel, and unjust enactments, I say, let it be done."* He became an example to Union soldiers in the Civil War, who sang a song about him. For years, Brown was accused of insanity by racist whites unwilling to understand his commitment to justice.

*Quoted in James H. Loewen, *Lies My Teacher Told Me* (New York: New Press, 1995), 168.

the boundaries or locations of these reservations. Many of them were historically nomadic, but the establishment of the reservations restricted their movement. What grew in their homeland did not necessarily grow in their new reservation. The dividing line also was not kept; as white settlers, the U.S.-Mexico War, the U.S. Civil War, and other forces encroached on the 95th meridian, the lands set aside for refugee Indians shrank farther. Only 30,000 Indians lived east of the Mississippi in 1844, a dramatic decrease from the 120,000 who lived there in 1820.[6]

Japanese Concentration Camps

The bombing of Pearl Harbor by Japanese warplanes shocked and outraged the American people—and led to another shameful period of forced migration and segregation. Anti-Japanese hysteria led to a number of organizations—such as the American Legions of California, Oregon, and Washington; the *Los Angeles Times*; and the Grower-Shipper Vegetable Association—to call for the removal of all those of Japanese descent.[7]

Attorney General Francis Biddle stated in a memo to President Franklin Roosevelt that evacuation of American citizens based on their racial categorization was determined to be unconstitutional.[8] In February 1942, FBI director J. Edgar Hoover determined that Japanese in the United States and Japanese Americans posed no real espionage threat. Despite this counsel, President Roosevelt signed Executive Order 9066 on February 19, 1942. General John DeWitt was authorized to remove all Americans of Japanese descent from the western states to be processed and relocated to inland concentration camps. Approximately 120,000 persons—men, women, and children—were moved from their homes. The United States also requested that Latin American governments deport over 2,200 persons of Japanese descent from Latin America to the United States to be interned and used for prisoner exchanges.[9] Families were told they had just a few days to sell all their belongings or entrust them to banks, friends, or neighbors. The shame of being seen as the enemy was multiplied as white people came to buy valuables, houses, and land for far less than their actual value. Despite the Alien Land Laws, which prohibited noncitizen ownership of land in the western United States, Japanese American families owned some lucrative farmland that was highly coveted by neighboring white farmers. Entire families left everything, bringing only what they could carry, and went first to evacuation centers, then to assembly centers. These assembly centers were in the horse and cattle stalls at such places as the fairgrounds in Puyallup, Washington, and the Santa Ana racetrack in California, made famous by Seabiscuit. They then were sent to live for three years in uninsulated barracks in various rural areas, where the family system was severely disrupted by a life without private space. People were not allowed to leave the camps unless accompanied by guards while providing labor to neighboring farms, or unless they were on their way to serve in the military. In contrast, the only people of German and Italian descent imprisoned within the United States were charged with specific acts of espionage.

Colonialism

As the United States spread west in its colonial expansion, white Americans began to encroach upon territory belonging to Mexicans, who had been there for generations. So many Americans were entering the territory known as Texas that the Mexican government requested an investigation into the influx.[10] Mexican citizens were divided on the presence of Americans, with some in support and some opposed. In 1830, Mexico made slavery illegal while also prohibiting any more American migration. Americans continued to cross the border as undocumented migrants. Stephen Austin, for whom the city of Austin, Texas, is named, framed the conflict as one "between a 'mongrel Spanish-Indian and negro race' and 'civilization and the Anglo-American race.'"[11] In 1836, tensions came to a head in a series of violent confrontations. American rebels barricaded themselves in the Alamo and fought an illegal war with Mexican troops. Mexican troops captured a nearby town and executed 400 Americans. In the rebuttal to this, Americans killed 630 Mexicans. Sam Houston forced General Santa Anna to hand Texas over to him as an independent republic. In the ensuing struggle between Mexico and the United States over the border of Texas with Mexico (whether it was the Rio Grande or the Rio Nueces), American soldiers killed Mexican civilians with

Manifest Destiny

As the "permanent Indian frontier" was crossed or encroached upon by U.S. soldiers going to fight Mexico in 1847, by white Easterners in the 1848 California gold rush, and by settlers going toward New Mexico and Oregon, U.S. lawmakers sought a way to justify this laxity of the borders. They invented the concept of Manifest Destiny, deciding that "Europeans and their descendants were ordained by destiny to rule all of America."* They were given license to rule Native Americans, as well as all their land and material goods. In 1850, Minnesota gained statehood and along with it, one hundred miles of the so-called permanent Indian frontier.†

*Dee Brown, *Bury My Heart at Wounded Knee: An Indian History of the American West*, 30th anniversary ed. (New York: Henry Holt & Co., 2001), 8.

†Ibid., 9.

impunity. In 1848, the United States defeated Mexico, and the Treaty of Guadalupe Hidalgo ceded half of Mexico to the United States, including all of California, New Mexico, Nevada, and parts of what are now Colorado, Arizona, and Utah.[12] Ashbel Smith declared that the "inferior must give way before the superior race."[13] Manifest Destiny thrived throughout this conquest, being used to prove that Mexicans and their descendants were unfit for the land and that Americans were meant to take over land previously inhabited by inferior races. This provided Americans with more land and a wealth of natural resources.

Neocolonialism

The Foraker Act in 1900 made Puerto Rican citizens into American citizens with very limited representation (a nonvoting commissioner to the U.S. House of Representatives) and imposed a civilian government designed by the United States, including a governor and executive council appointed by the U.S. president. This opened up Puerto Rico to neocolonial domination. With Puerto Rico a territory of the United States, American companies were able to move into Puerto Rico and were given significant tax incentives to do so. However, Puerto Rican companies were not allowed to operate in the United States. The limited representation of Puerto Rico to Washington, D.C., including the ineligibility of Puerto Ricans living on the island to vote in U.S. presidential elections, allowed any opposition to policies regarding or affecting Puerto Rico by those most affected to be ignored. In the early years of the U.S.-Puerto Rico relationship, the people of Puerto Rico voted against this particular arrangement but were overruled by the U.S. Congress. This laid the groundwork for pharmaceutical companies to enter and test drugs on the population. This testing included involuntary sterilizations of many Puerto Rican women. Although American pharmaceutical companies employed Puerto Ricans, most profits did not return to the island.

CHAPTER 5

1954–1973: MOVEMENT TIME — FROM OVERT TO COVERT

This chapter explores how social movements, along with landmark cases such as *Brown*, not only changed how people of color interacted with U.S. laws and policies, but also how these movements changed the ways racism was manifested: from overt and legally sanctioned policies to covert cultural and systemic racism, often invisible to the dominant society. The chapter raises the connected and interrelated nature of movements for justice. This period of massive social change, facilitated by movements that shared leadership and mutual inspiration, challenged and changed how racism and other forms of social evil were embedded in U.S. culture and the economy.

Rise of the Middle Class

Extending from 1946 into the 1950s, several factors resulted in the development of a white middle class in a way that left African Americans, in particular, behind. (The status of Latinos, Asian Americans, and Native Americans varied according to location and is less well documented.) What took place before the end of legal segregation laid the foundation for continued exclusion of African Americans after 1954, further cementing inequality that arose not out of intent, but from the continued impact of historical racism.

Congress passed the G.I. Bill at the end of World War II, providing such benefits as subsidized education and homeownership assistance to all veterans of the war. However, the ability of veterans to take advantage of the bill's provisions varied according to their race. White working-class and lower-class men were able to move up to the middle class thanks to subsidized higher education. African American men were unable to do the same, since educational opportunities were curtailed by legal segregation that allowed universities to refuse admission to African American applicants. This inability to obtain an education as easily as white men was compounded by a differential ability to purchase a home, the primary way in which people in the United States have been able to accrue wealth that can be passed down to succeeding generations.

As soldiers returned from service and settled down in homes and with families, white flight began with a vengeance. Whites were able to move out to the burgeoning suburbs thanks to a number of factors. The first was lending practices that privileged white applicants over African American applicants. Redlining, the practice by which banks drew lines on maps between neighborhoods to delineate those neighborhoods in which they would lend money to buyers to purchase houses, and restrictive covenants, in which buyers agreed not to sell a house to anyone from a particular group (such as Jews, blacks, or Asians), cemented residential segregation. Whites were able to move out to the suburbs. African Americans were led to city residences,

The Movements

During the period this chapter spans, social movements dominated the United States: the civil rights movement, the black power movement (including the Black Panthers and the Nation of Islam), the American Indian movement, the Chicano movement, the farmworkers movement, the women's liberation or second-wave feminist movement, the gay rights movement, the yellow power movement, the antiwar movement, the Puerto Rican freedom movement, the peace movement, and the environmental justice movement. Our understanding of these movements is often limited by the linear ways in which the education system in the United States approaches the teaching of history. However, these movements emerged simultaneously, often inspiring and informing each other. Leaders such as Ella Baker, Grace Lee Boggs, Yuri Kochiyama, Angela Davis, Dolores Huerta, and Myles Horton stood in solidarity, informing and shaping each other's movements.

black suburbs, or particular lower-value neighborhoods by a practice called steering. Steering takes place when real estate agents show prospective buyers only certain houses, a practice that persists to the present day. Until the 1980s, blockbusting contributed to residential segregation, as real estate agents encouraged white homeowners to sell their houses as African American families moved into a particular neighborhood, citing the likelihood that home values would fall as a result of integration.

Growth of the suburbs was encouraged by the further development of interstate highways, first built on a large scale during the war to move military equipment and people safely across distances. As the interstates developed, more suburban growth took place as a result of easier movement between suburbs and the city core. Urban renewal, a term used to describe black displacement, interstate development, and the destruction of viable communities allowed this movement between (largely white) suburbs and (largely black) urban cores. As Tom Lewis notes, James Baldwin "characterized urban renewal more caustically as 'Negro removal.'"[1] The Riverfront Expressway in New Orleans effectively turned a family-friendly, economically vibrant black community—and the center of black Mardi Gras in New Orleans—into the street below the elevated Interstate 10. By the early 1960s, it became clear that the way of least resistance for interstate construction was a black community, as residents did not have sufficient access to

---

The Resistance: Yuri Kochiyama

Yuri Kochiyama was imprisoned at the Japanese concentration camp in Jerome, Arkansas. Over time, her religious and political views led her to join what she called "The Movement," a series of struggles for freedom for Puerto Rican and Black Panther political prisoners, for black civil rights and black power, and in support of civil liberties and victims of war. Kochiyama tells a story of what evangelist E. Stanley Jones said during a speech at the Santa Anita Assembly Center, one of the stops along the way to internment in 1942. He said, "It doesn't matter so much what happens 'to' you as what happens 'inside' of you—and what you do 'after' it happens." Thus, life's blows, whether they come in the form of an evacuation experience that struck the Japanese Americans collectively or a breakup that jolts people individually, need not be knockout punches but just experiences to grow on.*

*Diane C. Fujino, *Heartbeat of Struggle: The Revolutionary Life of Yuri Kochiyama* (Minneapolis: University of Minnesota Press, 2005), 50.

city government and its power structure. Highway engineer Robert Moses "each year leveled the homes of tens of thousands of blacks to make way for ever more miles of expressways around and through New York."[2] The G.I. Bill, white flight and the housing boom, the expansion of higher education to more working-class and lower-class white men, and legal segregation laid the groundwork for a booming white middle class and an African American community without access to the same benefits, further entrenching inequality between black and white. The outcomes of these laws endure into the twenty-first century, resulting in racist outcomes of institutional policies not intended to be racist. David Roediger quotes *Ebony* magazine's analysis of a Frank Sinatra movie called *The House I Live In*, about white immigrants who organized around issues of homeownership and discrimination: "Never will a white man in America have to live in a ghetto hemmed in by court-approved legal documents, trapped by an invisible wall of hate much more formidable than the Siegfried line."[3]

We Shall Overcome: Movements for Change Enter the Stage

In 1954, fifty-eight years after the Supreme Court's landmark decision in *Plessy v. Ferguson* established apartheid in the United States, the *Brown* decision disavowed "separate but equal," ruling that *de jure* (in principle) racial segregation was a violation of the equal protection clause of the Fourteenth Amendment of the Constitution. This ruling set the stage for the passing of the Civil Rights Act of 1964 and the Voting Rights Act in 1965. Furthermore, the power of the *Brown* decision rippled through U.S. society and culture, fueling the smoldering coals of a resistance movement that would change history.

Most people identify Rosa Parks's 1955 act of civil disobedience in a Montgomery bus as the seminal event of the civil rights movement. While the actions that led Parks to challenge the racial segregation in public transportation are not to be diminished, resistance to the U.S. system of apartheid began decades before. From the founding of the Howard University Law School to the establishment of the NAACP Legal Defense Fund; from the Harlem Renaissance to the protest songs taught and learned at the Highlander Center in Knoxville, Tennessee; from the words of W. E. B. Du Bois to those of Howard Thurman; resistance to racism has been a powerful builder of people.

In 1910, the NAACP began publishing *The Crisis*. In its opening issue, W. E. B. Du Bois wrote,

> Some good friends of the cause we represent fear agitation. They say: "Do not agitate—do not make noise; work." They add, "Agitation is destructive or at best negative—what is wanted is positive constructive work." Such honest critics mistake the function of agitation . . . agitation is a necessary evil to tell of the ills of the Suffering. Without it many a nation has been lulled to false security and preened itself with virtues it did not possess.[4]

With agitation in mind, the social movements that came to dominate and change power relations in the United States moved into the limelight in the decades following the *Brown* decision. The actions of these movements pushed racism to assume new, less discernable forms.

Ensuring the Maintenance of the Status Quo: COINTELPRO

The Counterintelligence Program of the Federal Bureau of Investigation, or COINTELPRO, operated between 1956 and 1971. Established to protect national security, prevent violence, and maintain the existing social and political order, COINTELPRO sought to "disrupt and neutralize" movement groups and individuals perceived as threats to the United States. The emergence of COINTELPRO in a landscape where social movements were seeking to agitate and disrupt the status quo had serious consequences for the FBI and the leaders of the movements. Under COINTELPRO, techniques the FBI had used against "hostile" foreign agents were used against American citizens. Through covert action, COINTELPRO sought to influence the political choices and social values of movements by infiltrating them with *agents provocateurs*. Five groups became the primary targets for COINTELPRO: "Communist Party, USA" (1956–1971), "Socialist Workers Party" (1961–1969), "White Hate Group" (1964–1971), "Black Nationalist—Hate Group" (1967–1971), and "New Left" (1968–1971). It is important to note that the FBI defined these so vaguely that many citizens who were simply exercising their rights of speech and civil disobedience became targets of the program, as their actions were perceived to be threats to domestic tranquility. For example, the Southern Christian Leadership Conference was a target of this program, along with Martin Luther King Jr.[5]

Is that Racism? New Codified Language Emerges

As the end of this period approached, the manifestations of racism became covertly embedded in our national language. Words and phrases such as *welfare queen, domestic terrorist, Affirmative Action hire, deadbeat dads, generational poverty, urban underclass, permanently unemployed, model minority, wetback, illegal alien, spy,* and *urban renewal*, among others, substituted for overtly racist language, leaving the hearer uncertain of the speaker's intent. Words and phrases like the ones just named have entered our national lexicon connected to images that reinforce for us the inferior, criminal, and threatening nature of people of color.

Consider President George H. W. Bush's 1988 campaign ad in which Massachusetts inmate William Horton, a black man convicted for murder and rape, was frequently mentioned by President Bush as a "terrorizer of innocent people."[6] William Horton was serving a life sentence for murder (without possibility for parole) and participated in the state of Massachusetts' program of weekend furloughs for prisoners. Horton did not return from one of his weekends and subsequently committed assault, armed robbery, and rape. The Bush campaign ad had four different incarnations, each using the Horton case as an example of what happens when politicians are "weak on crime." It had profound implications on the 1988 presidential election. As reported in an in-depth study of the ad conducted by Brown University,

The spots aroused racial fears as well. Owing to Horton's visage, made clear in "Weekend Passes" and network news coverage, race was an obvious factor in how voters saw the crime spree. After all, Republicans had picked the perfect racial crime, that of a black felon raping a white woman. Experimental research drawing on the Horton case demonstrated that viewers saw the story more as a case of race than crime. According to researchers, subjects who were exposed to news broadcasts about the Horton case responded in racial terms. The ad mobilized whites' racial prejudice, not their worries about crime. Viewers became much more likely to feel negatively about blacks in general after having heard the details of the case.[7]

> ### Connecting Movements: Second-Wave Feminism and Women's Liberation
>
> Another movement in the 1960s and 1970s with great social significance was the feminist movement. Typically thought to have been galvanized with the 1963 publication of Betty Friedan's *The Feminine Mystique*, women began to organize. The legal issues that saw change in this era were pay equity, equality in education, and extending affirmative-action rights to women. Significant social change took place around attitudes regarding women and their place at work, in society, and in the home.

Most recently, Representative Harold Ford Jr. from Tennessee experienced the power of attack ads. In 2006, supporters of his opponent ran an ad depicted in this way by Taylor Marsh of the *Huffington Post*:

> The ad Howell produced . . . reaches into the deep, dark, dirty message of the south we are all trying to leave to history, resurrecting the racial prejudice one more time to get his client elected. The ad is complete with a naked blonde winking into the camera as she asks Harold to "call me." The ad is pure race baiting, bringing to mind the image of an old stereotype of a black man dating a blonde woman.[8]

Some race-baiting uses language that, on its face, is innocuous while obscuring the ways in which communities of color are impacted by racism. On January 6, 1966, six months after the unrest in Watts, the *New York Times Sunday Magazine* ran an article with the title "Success Story, Japanese American Style."[9] *U.S. News & World Report* followed suit that same year after urban unrest during the summer of 1966. This presentation of what is commonly referred to as the "model minority" myth coincided with urban unrest by mostly African Americans and with post-1965 immigration reform–induced migration of highly skilled workers from Asia.[10] Frank Wu describes how the author of the *New York Times* piece, William Peterson, wrote his statements almost in pairs, with "each commendation of Asian Americans . . . paired off against a reprimand of African Americans."[11] Stereotyping Asian Americans as successful over and against stereotypes of African Americans as not successful hides the economic and social diversity within groups of people of color. African Americans and Asian Americans alike span the economic spectrum.

As *de jure* segregation became illegal, racism continued as the middle class increased dramatically in size but disproportionately included white Americans, reinforcing an enduring wealth gap between white and black. Language, culture, and legal precedent changed, and racism moved from overt to covert. However, significant resistance that crossed class, race, gender, and sexual orientation was created by overlapping movements for justice and identity that forced sweeping social change. This resistance — and covert racism — have moved us toward contemporary racism.

CHAPTER 6

―――――――― ⚭ ――――――――

1973–PRESENT: POST-MOVEMENT TIME— RACISM REDEFINED

We in the United States have reason to be hopeful about the state of racism in our nation. After all, we are increasingly diverse, and our leadership as a country is beginning to represent that diversity. Representation in government still lags behind, however. As of 2015, the U.S. Senate included only six people of color: two African Americans (Cory Booker, D-NJ; Tim Scott, R-SC), one Asian American (Mazie Hirono, D-HI), and three Latinos (Ted Cruz, R-TX; Bob Menendez, D-NJ; Marco Rubio, R-FL).[1] In addition, there are only twenty women and not a single Native American.[2] If the Senate were truly representative of the United States' racial and gender makeup based on 2013 demographics, there would be thirty-seven people of color and fifty-one women.[3]

Representation is also an issue on corporate boards, with Asian American men in particular disproportionately absent despite their presence in the professional workforce. Some church groups have the opposite problem. For example, despite having several leaders of color, the Presbyterian Church (U.S.A.) remains overwhelmingly white. Media portrayals of various groups of people of color leave much to be desired. African American and Latino men are disproportionately part of the prison population. Immigration is a continuing vehicle for cultural racism. Neocolonialism in Asia and Latin America serve as contemporary extensions of the doctrine of Manifest Destiny. This chapter covers just a few contemporary manifestations of the ways in which racism continues to be present in everyday life.

Criminalization and Legalized Disenfranchisement

The last legal obstacles to full citizenship for African Americans were eliminated with the 1965 Voting Rights Act, a key provision of which was overturned in 2013 by the U.S. Supreme Court.[4] Citizenship implies full participation in society, including voting. This is not true for people who have been convicted of felonies. Almost 25 percent of all African American men in their thirties had been to prison by 2003,[5] and 13 percent of African American men are ineligible to vote due to felony convictions.[6] In addition, African Americans receive longer prison sentences for drug crimes because sentencing varies based not on the crime committed but on the ways in which people of different races are charged (with possession, or with possession with the intent to distribute) and on the types of drugs. For example, crack cocaine is cheaper and more likely to be used by African Americans than powder cocaine, which is more likely to be used by white people. Users of powder cocaine need to possess 100 times more cocaine than do users of crack cocaine in order to receive the same sentence. Because of the differences in sentencing, the impact of incarceration is much greater on poor people of color from urban areas.[7]

The criminal justice system impacts the way African Americans in particular experience citizenship. Convicted felons who have served their time in prison and completed probation remain ineligible to vote in most states. Only Maine and Vermont allow prison inmates the right to vote.[8] Thirty-five states prohibit felons on parole from voting. Given the disproportionate numbers of African American and Latino men in prison, and the disproportionate sentences given to people of color, we might say that the result of these laws is the restriction of citizenship based on race.

Anti-Arab Racism, Immigration, and Neocolonialism

The war on terror, along with a continuing focus on extremists in, from, or with ancestry from the Middle East, has shaped the contemporary racial imagination. In recent years, mainstream movies have portrayed Arabic-speaking villains without families, fear, or compassion. A pre-9/11 example of this is the 1994 movie *True Lies*, in which several Arabic-speaking male characters of undetermined national origin plot to use a nuclear weapon if the United States does not meet their demands. Positive portrayals by Arab Americans actors are rarely of Arab American characters. For example, the title character in the 2002–2009 TV series *Monk*, assumed to be white, was played by Tony Shalhoub, an American of Lebanese descent.

Are Arabs a race? As comedian Dean Obeidallah stated on the Axis of Evil Comedy Tour, "I used to be a white guy. After September 11, I became an Arab."[9] Arab Americans are considered white in the legal racial construction of the

United States. Arabs, a classification often conflated with Muslims, have been more prominently racialized since 9/11. The post-9/11 discourse on evil by mainstream leaders conflate Islam, terrorism, and Arabs, despite efforts by Presidents George W. Bush and Barack Obama to distinguish between Islam and extremist violence. In 2004, House majority leader Tom DeLay gave a speech in which the word *evil* was used almost twenty times to describe the so-called Arab world.[10] As English professor Steven Salaita points out, *terrorism* is a "highly subjective term and its subjectivity has been used to highlight Arab violence disproportionately while comparable American and Israeli violence is disregarded."[11] Anti-Arab racism is reflected in U.S. culture in the media, popular culture, and the Bush-era discourse of the "war on terror." After 9/11, Muslim communities reported increased difficulty with securing

---

Resistance: Spoken Word and Comedy

Spoken-word groups such as Yellow Rage and the Taco Shop Poets and artists such as Marlon Esguerra bring their cultural and racial experiences to light while critiquing racism in the United States. Comedians Ahmed Ahmed, Maz Jobrani, Dean Obeidallah, and Aron Kader brought their Arab American and Iranian American experiences together to create the Axis of Evil Comedy Tour. Negin Farsad, Dean Obeidallah, Aron Kader, Preacher Moss, Kareem Omary, Maysoon Zayid, and Omar Elba star in *The Muslims Are Coming!*, a documentary about Muslim American comedians touring the United States to fight Islamophobia. They and Korean American comedian Margaret Cho in her "I'm the One That I Want" comedy tour have provided a strong counterpoint to dominant social narratives about people of color from the perspective of people of color.

permits to build mosques for worship. Of course, not all Arabs are Muslim. Not all Muslims are Arabs. Not all Arabs or Muslims are terrorists. In fact, adherents of Islam span a wide theological and political spectrum, similar to the spectrum of practicing Christians. This conflation in the American imagination of Arab/Muslim/terrorist creates a racialized category whose members are assumed to participate in destructive behavior.

After September 11, 2001, hate crimes against people who looked Arab increased dramatically. Between September 11 and September 13, the Council on American-Islamic Relations received over three hundred reports of harassment and abuse. The first murder was of a South Asian man in Arizona, believed to have been targeted because of his turban and long beard, which are characteristic of Sikh adherents.[12] The aftermath of September 11 included voluntary registration by men from twenty majority-Muslim and majority-Arab countries.[13] These voluntary registrations resulted in hundreds of men disappearing for months at a time, thanks to the government's "hold until cleared" policy.[14] Many were deported, and most were held in detention without the ability to contact their families.

The debate regarding immigration reform and enforcement has cycled through both cultural and systemic racism. Vigilantes on the border between the United States and Mexico engage in anti-Latino violence, while they believe they are assisting the U.S. Border Patrol in finding and turning back people crossing the border. A more recent phenomenon surfaced in which mostly white youth go looking for "Mexicans." This is known as "beaner hunting."[15] Since 1994, border enforcement and the construction of a wall along portions of the U.S.-Mexico border have forced immigrants into more hazardous terrain. Such measures have made these crossings more dangerous, and those who cross successfully are more likely to stay longer and to bring their families because going home for a visit is now far more difficult.[16] The naturalization process involves quotas that do not reflect colonial histories or current flows of migration. Colonization has resulted in later immigration of previous colonial subjects (e.g., Indian and Pakistani migration to Great Britain, Filipino migration to the United States). Quotas established in 1976 limited the number of people who may enter the United States from other countries in the Western Hemisphere each year at 20,000.

Countries such as Cuba, Puerto Rico, and the Philippines have experienced the United States as a neocolonizing power. Neocolonialism describes economic control or dominance of one country over another and may or may not include control over the government. The United States continues to assert neocolonial control over various countries in Asia and Latin America. What does this have to do with racism in the United States? After all, our relationships to other countries are not racialized, are they?

The doctrine of Manifest Destiny was developed as a justification for the United States to reach into Mexican territories. The superiority complex it was based on filtered into U.S. foreign policy. The Iran-Contra Affair is one such example of U.S. interference colored by Manifest Destiny. The United States sold arms to Iran, without regard for the eventual cost this might have for Iranians, in exchange for U.S. hostages being held in Iran. The proceeds from the arms sales went to fund the pro–U.S. government contra rebels in Nicaragua. The fight between the contras and the ruling Sandinistas was an internal struggle over power and forms of government; U.S. funding of the contras became neocolonial interference. The Sandinistas were Marxist, and the United States has a history of finding ways to subvert leftist movements in other countries in order to support capitalism, an economic system more beneficial to the United States.

The Resistance: Japanese American Protest Against Muslim Detentions

Arab and South Asian immigrants detained after September 11 found that their situation was not viewed in isolation. Their detentions, which typically resulted in no charges or convictions beyond proving the Muslim faith of those detained, resonated with the Japanese American community. Japanese American organizations spoke out against the detentions without warrant as stemming from the same racism that imprisoned 120,000 people of Japanese descent during World War II. The children of Gordon Hirabayashi, Fred Korematsu, and Minoru Yasui (three men who were interned and filed a case against the government) filed an amicus brief on behalf of Arab and South Asian immigrants detained after September 11, arguing similarities with the internment experiences of Japanese Americans and that the equal protection clauses in the Constitution ought to be applied in such cases.*

*"Descendents of Japanese American Internees File Amicus Brief in Support of Muslim Immigrants," Center for Constitutional Rights press release, http://ccrjustice.org/newsroom/press-releases/descendents-japanese-american-internees-file-amicus-brief-support-muslim-imm.

The Level Playing Field and Multiculturalism

We hold onto the myth of meritocracy, the belief that ours is a system in which people gain positions based on their talent and not on their wealth, connections, class status, racial and cultural background, or other measures of power and privilege. This is founded on a belief that we all begin on a level playing field, that resources are distributed equally, and that earnings are based solely on a person's merit. Part of this myth is woven together with the belief that affirmative action is no longer necessary.

President Obama's nomination of Sonia Sotomayor to the Supreme Court evoked a frightening array of criticisms due to her status as a woman of color. Surely she, as a product of affirmative action, was less qualified than other possible candidates. (In fact, she had more experience as a judge than all other nominees throughout U.S. history.) *The Nation* accused Curt Levey of the Committee for Justice of repeating "unsourced accusations . . . that Sotomayor is an 'intellectual lightweight' who was 'picked because she was a woman and Hispanic.'"[17]

This narrative was purported to be part of a larger and perfectly valid exploration of her fitness to be appointed to the Supreme Court. By comparison, however, Chief Justice John Roberts was questioned primarily about his positions, beliefs, and prior job history, not his race or gender. The line of questioning regarding Sotomayor, focusing on her identity as a determining factor of her competence and her qualifications, was quite different.

Appointments to the Supreme Court such as Clarence Thomas and Sonia Sotomayor have lifted up elements of the ways in which multiculturalism can be racist. The only way these appointments will succeed in not changing the system is if the individuals share enough of the values of the U.S. judicial system that they will not change it. The attacks against Sotomayor may have been a manifestation of the fear that her appointment would change the status quo, as the defenders of the system did not see her as someone who would allow the U.S. judicial system to remain much as it is.

Multiculturalism lifts up racial and other differences and views them as making valuable contributions to education or the workforce. Racist multiculturalism, which came into force in the 1980s, perpetuates racism by seeking to make institutions look good without committing to changing the status quo. The assumption is if a person of color is placed in a white system, the system is free of its racism. But every institution has layers to its identity. The easiest layer to change is personnel. The deepest and most difficult layer to change is mission. Racist multiculturalism only seeks to bring diversity at the level of personnel and maybe programs; the status quo and power relationships established around the mission remain unchanged. Without any shift in the culture of the institution or its policies, racist multiculturalism aims to manage and control diversity and its impact on the organization. It is posed as the end of the journey.

In contrast, antiracist multiculturalism aims to transform an institution's relationship to its diverse communities and seeks to share power evenly among different people. Antiracist multiculturalism sees its approach as a step on the path to becoming the beloved community and understands that it is not yet an embodiment of the beloved community. This approach to multiculturalism has the self-awareness to examine and change each layer of the organization as part of its antiracist commitment. Only if the presence of people of color on the Supreme Court were to drastically change rulings made by the Supreme Court, or if the presence of people of color in Congress were to change how the United States defines and processes legal questions, would there be a dramatic departure toward antiracist multiculturalism. If those who appoint, approve, or vote into office people of color understand that this is one step toward a more just society around issues of race and class, it may be possible that the representation of people of color in high-profile positions can be a part of a larger vision for antiracist multiculturalism. If President Obama is the only person of color to serve as the president of the

United States, we know his presidency played into racist multiculturalism.

Conclusion

Racism from 1973 until now has multiple manifestations, some of which were explored in this chapter. As Christians, we are called in our baptism to a new life. We engage in relationship with God. We live in broken systemic relationships that belie our life of faith. If we are to engage in the healing of this world, we are greatly helped by a historical understanding of how this system of racism developed in the United States.

PART II

ISSUES OF RACISM TODAY

CHAPTER 7

DID OBAMA'S ELECTION
END RACISM?

It was a remarkable moment in Grant Park on Election Day in 2008 when the announcement was made that Obama had been elected president. Everyone at the park had been preparing for a really long night. And then it was done. Barack Hussein Obama had been elected president of the United States of America.

Thousands of people hugged, kissed, and cried in the crisp night air. Obama supporters had done something that few thought possible, with work put in by countless volunteers and many making small donations to give a massive financial boost to a young black senator from Illinois.

Something changed fundamentally about the United States that day.

While the historic election night party in Grant Park and the crowded Washington Mall on a cold, clear Inauguration Day in January remain an indelible turning point in the history of the United States, race relations and racism seem to many worse than they were before his election.

The more astute observers of President Obama understood that he was a pragmatic leader and that every president faces resistance. But even those who work on issues of racism have been taken aback by the sheer amount of hateful resistance that has distinguished his presidency. From the emergence of groups such as the Tea Party, the wild increase in gun sales in the days after the election, the debates around the legitimacy of Obama's citizenship, and the questions regarding Obama's religious affiliation, the ideology of white supremacy has reared its ugly head throughout his terms in office.[1]

The election of this man was indeed a turning point and was hailed by countries around the world. Children have grown up only knowing an African American president. Young people of color know that it is possible to aspire to that elected office, with a real example of someone who made it there.

Why hasn't the Obama presidency meant an age of renewed racial reconciliation, of better racial relationships in our country? The years 2008 through 2016 saw change in race relations but not the unmitigated improvement many hoped was the reason behind Barack Obama's election.

Real Change during Obama's presidency

President Obama was elected to the White House with a platform to bring about change and hope. In many ways, however, race relations in the United States seemed to be worse near the end of his presidency.

The housing collapse of 2008, which began before Obama's election and reverberated throughout his presidency, revealed longstanding predatory lending practices that impacted people of color more than they did white people.[2] The crisis widened the racial wealth gap. During the recovery between 2009 and 2011, white wealth began to recover while black wealth continued its precipitous decline. From 2010 to 2013, the median wealth of white households increased from $138,600 to $141,900. In the same period, the median wealth of black households fell 33.7 percent from $16,600 to $11,000, while the median wealth of Latino households fell 14.3 percent, from $16,000 to $13,700.[3] Communities that are predominantly Hispanic were hit hardest by the crisis, with home values falling the furthest.[4]

In 2013, the Supreme Court eroded the civil rights guarantees of the Voting Rights Act when it struck down the provision requiring states, counties, and municipalities with a history of voting rights violations to seek federal approval for changes in voting laws.[5]

Since the death of Michael Brown in 2014, the level of police brutality experienced by African Americans and Native Americans—the communities most likely to be killed by law enforcement officers in the United States—are under heightened scrutiny.[6]

The Obama administration is responsible for widespread long-term detention of unauthorized immigrants and record-high rates of deportations.[7]

White Supremacy Unshaken

Barack Obama was not elected to be the president of a racially just nation. He was elected to the presidency of a neocolonial nation constantly at war, with a record of confining and eliminating its indigenous population and incarcerating proportionately more black people than South Africa at the height of apartheid.[8] He was elected to be the president of a nation where corporations have rights as persons but a person's rights to protest or to stop the actions of a corporation are limited.

Barack Obama wasn't elected on a platform of radical change. He believed in technical solutions to social problems, as evidenced by his education policy and its emphasis on testing, the reaffirmation of the No Child Left Behind Act, and the institution of Race to the Top grants. As an African American, President Obama made history by being the first man elected president who was not white. But he did not get elected necessarily to challenge the patterns of white supremacy that have always been at the heart of what the United States is.

In her essay "Heteropatriarchy and the Three Pillars of White Supremacy," Andrea Smith discusses the foundations of white supremacy in the United States.[9] The first of the pillars that undergird it is genocide. Specific to the United States is the genocide of the peoples on whose land this nation is built. The strategy of that logic is settler colonialism. The United States began as a settler colonial nation in a so-called discovered land, and it possessed that land fully from coast to coast. Those who settled the territory that became the United States came under the belief that it had been set up by God as a city on a hill, to be a place of security and democracy for all those they considered human. The cost of that, of course, was the genocide of indigenous peoples. The number of Native American deaths by disease and warfare are staggering. Our national mythology likes to think that this is the result of contact with Europeans, that it is somehow an accident of new people encountering each other. But the United States engaged in and continues to engage in policies against Native Americans that are genocidal. All one has to do is consider the Native American boarding schools that began in the 1870s and ran well into the twentieth century. Built for the strict purpose of "saving the man by killing the Indian," these schools were dedicated to the cultural genocide of a people.

Smith argues that the second pillar of white supremacy is slavery. The United States is built upon the sweat of enslaved persons. Slavery has been a major source of economic prosperity for this nation and was built into the capitalist model used in the United States. This system objectifies human beings and the earth in order to extract their resources and their labor for the benefit of those who are in control of society.

Therein lie two of the inherent contradictions of this nation that proclaims itself to be a place where all people can pursue happiness. Two of its peoples—native people and enslaved Africans—were systematically exploited and killed. Their humanity was stripped from them as they were removed from the land and enslaved for the economic benefit of others. Native Americans and forcibly removed Africans were not savages or heathens as the European settlers claimed. It was the settler culture that turned people into savages.

Finally, says Smith, the third pillar of white supremacy is what she calls orientalism. Here she builds on the work of Edward Said. *Orientalism* as used here is seen as the creation of perpetual foreignness. This is a kind of otherness where individuals and nations are considered foreign. Their foreignness is seen as a threat to the United States and must be suppressed and controlled through force. Groups, such as American Muslims, are the objects of surveillance in order to ensure that American interests are preserved and maintained.[10]

This practice of suspecting groups of non-white people as permanent potential threats helps explain the way the United States viewed (or continues to view) Native American reservations, World War II–era Japanese internment camps, Guantanamo Bay, and Abu Ghraib. It details the

U.S. need to control all those who are seen as a threat to national security as defined by the dominant society, to put them in places while those in power determine what to do to them. Behind the detention of Japanese Americans in World War II was the idea that these were people who could never be absorbed into the general population and therefore were forever suspect, that these people needed to be watched constantly in the event that they might plot against the nation of their birth, the nation in which they chose to work, live, and raise families.

White supremacy, argues Smith, is a series of logics that make meaning out of our current reality for those who have internalized it. It is a way of understanding the world, the relationship of this nation relative to every other place in this earth, and the earth itself. This worldview helps explain why the Obama presidency does not signify the end of American racism and has not made major steps toward racial reconciliation.

White supremacy is inclusive of but not limited to the existence of the people in white hoods who adhere to beliefs about white superiority. White supremacy is a worldview, a frame through which reality is seen. It is that frame that we have to begin to contend with. It is that frame that is dangerous. It is that frame that all of us participate in.

For a conversation about racism in the United States to be productive, it has to acknowledge that it is white supremacy in all its forms that continues to make racism thrive. Moreover, such a conversation requires understanding how the systems and institutions of the United States give form and function to logics of white supremacy and thus discriminate systemically against communities of color. Efforts to end racism will remain focused on interpersonal relationships and fail to see that all human relationships are mediated by institutions unless we learn to see how racism, as a proxy of white supremacy, is carried out by systems and institutions.

Examples of White Supremacy

A visible sign that systemic racism is alive and well is the U.S. prison and immigrant detention system. This system increasingly utilizes for-profit privatized prisons. Private prisons get contracts to house and contain inmates with a minimum residency requirement. This shifts the incentive of the criminal justice system away from the restoration of people to the community toward a profit motive based on length of stay. The system isn't interested in human restoration. It is interested in how much money it will produce from each of the bodies that is incarcerated.

Another sign is the current culture of policing. While many in the United States have seemed taken aback by the levels of police brutality reported in the media, communities of color have always known this to be their reality. Police forces began as instruments of the wealthy class to protect their interests. They were used for decades to control and terrorize racial communities. They have never been systematically retrained to protect the poor and people of color. Policing in the United States is also increasingly militarized, thanks to the country's prolonged participation in war and the distribution of free surplus military equipment.[11] Paul Chappell, a former military officer and now a peace activist, names dehumanization and objectification as a training requirement for soldiers engaging in warfare.[12] People aren't people; they are threats that need to be neutralized. People aren't communities; they are potential threats, potential criminals, so the approach to the community isn't one of service, but one of control and containment.

Yet another sign that white supremacy is thriving is the increase in nativism during the Obama presidency. Nativism describes the historical movements within American society in which the United States has turned inward. It is the idea that only those who are "native" belong to this land. Ironically, it tends to be inclusive only of white people, even though only Native Americans in the continental United States, Alaska, and Hawaii and Mexicans in the Southwest could ever claim to be native to this land. Nativism has fueled movements such as the Tea Party and has driven would-be politicians such as Donald Trump to call for the elimination of birthright citizenship. Nativism is what drove Ted Cruz to publicly renounce his dual Canadian citizenship in order to prove that he is, in fact, an American. Nativism is what has driven so-called birthers to contend throughout the Obama presidency that President Obama is not truly an American citizen. It inspired hundreds of protestors to show up at the exit of a detention center at the border to prevent children from being given fair treatment by U.S. immigration officials.[13] It is nativism that drives the vigilantes who patrol the U.S.-Mexico border and who forget that the natives actually are the Mexicans whose land was stolen by the U.S. government.

The election of an African American man cannot overturn deep historical patterns that undergird the racism and the xenophobia of our society.

Color-Blindness and Postracialism

Millennials are the most ethnically and racially diverse generation ever born. We love to exalt them as models for how to not just engage but transcend the need for intentional conversations about racism. Yet, reports Scott Clement, "over 3 in 10 white millennials believe blacks to be lazier or less hardworking than whites, and a similar number say lack of motivation is a reason why they are less financially well off as a group."[14] This generation is as embedded in the racist logics of this nation as the rest of us, but with one added difficulty: they were taught that to see race and name its power was a form of racism. The ideology of color-blindness and misguided postracialism are their stumbling block. Color-blindness tells us that people can be unique individuals, judged on their own merits and operating outside of the markers of race. This is a myth. The United States has always been defined by the racial categories that arise from the ideology of white supremacy.

Ideological frameworks such as color-blindness and postracialism serve to obfuscate the ways in which race and racism operate in this society. They create alternative narratives that push our gaze away from white supremacy and toward specific individual behaviors, to notions of meritocracy and individual achievements, to affirm narratives of American possibility and American exceptionalism.

The idea that we are able to see each other as children of God, measuring each other only based on the content of our character, is the kind of thinking that becomes dangerous for conversations around race, because it individualizes all social problems. This thinking leads us to believe the real problem isn't that we have a racist system of imprisonment for profit but that bad individuals wasted their opportunities and chose not to take advantage of the promise that this country represents. This thinking says the problem is not that we have an educational system that offers subpar education to children of color but that the parents and the breakdown of the family is the problem.

The system of postracial color-blindness frames police brutality as a problem of people who don't know their place. People don't know how to respect the role of police officers who are risking their lives on a daily basis. The problem is not police officers; the problem is that people are criminal. It isn't about police targeting people of color. We don't have a racial system in the United States. The police officers don't see race. All human beings matter after all. The evidence, of course, proves the contrary.

The consequence of the postracial color-blind ideology built over the last thirty years is that we have lost the capacity to talk about the depth and complexity of racism in the United States. We use terms like *white supremacy* to identify the behavior of individual people but not to describe an ideology that undergirds our history and our culture. We don't have the capacity to hear what people of color are telling us about their experiences without personalizing it, feeling attacked, and becoming defensive.

We lack language that allows us to understand even our own stories of racialization. If race is not real, if we are not to see race, we are unable to recognize how we are brought into a racial identity and how it impacts the possibilities available to us. That inability to have language means that we are unable to have a healthy conversation.

Conclusion

Systemic racism is so embedded in U.S. law, culture, and mores that even the historic election of the first black president does not change the racist reality of the country. One of the challenges of working for racial justice is that it will not happen overnight. The ways in which white supremacy is embedded in every single social institution in U.S. society makes bringing about racial equity a task for the long term. In a young society accustomed to quick fixes, we want things to happen immediately. In a society deeply committed to the pursuit of comfort, we want transformation without discomfort or a change in the status quo.

People want change to come overnight. And they quickly grow tired of the struggle. We are willing to show up to a march, a demonstration, or a sit-in. We like our picture taken and posted on Facebook, but the work of ending racism will go on long after the current outpouring of protest and demonstration. This will not stop the minimization and destruction of life. Much more will be required.

We Christians are called, through our faith and the outpouring of God's love that is Jesus Christ, to work actively to dismantle any and all ideological systems that deny the dignity of people and are contrary to God's will for creation. Racism in the United States is primary among systems of oppression. Dismantling systemic racism begins with small steps: educating ourselves, acquiring the language for the struggle, building our capacity to think systemically, and refusing to ignore the racism that is right in front of us. It does require, however, big steps. Institutions such as the church have to examine and interrogate their own complicity in the logics of white supremacy that feed systemic racism even as they call the nation to structural transformation. Will the church have the will to act?

CHAPTER 8

DO SEGREGATED
CHURCHES IMPLY RACISM?

In an interview at Western Michigan University in 1963, Martin Luther King Jr. spoke about segregation in the church. He was responding to a question about whether or not he thought integration should occur in the church before it took place in public venues such as schools, department stores, and public parks. He said,

> We must face the fact that in America, the church is still the most segregated major institution in America. At 11:00 on Sunday morning when we stand and sing and Christ has no east or west, we stand at the most segregated hour in this nation. This is tragic. Nobody of honesty can overlook this. Now, I'm sure that if the church had taken a stronger stand all along, we wouldn't have many of the problems that we have. The first way that the church can repent, the first way that it can move out into the arena of social reform is to remove the yoke of segregation from its own body.[1]

Several points in this statement are helpful in exploring racial segregation in the church. First, King was disappointed with the hypocrisy of the church, which sang about the oneness of Christ in worship yet actively engaged in racial segregation every week and did not take a more active role in challenging the ideology of racism. Second, he believed that the church played a role in the proliferation of segregation. Third, he believed that the church should repent of its sins by ceasing to practice racial segregation in worship.

Is King correct about the church helping to proliferate racism? Is it in the best interest of all concerned for the church to become integrated? What does true integration look like? Before we can respond to these questions, it is important to understand a bit more about the impetus of racial ideology and the history of racial segregation in churches in the United States.

Origin of Racial Ideology

The United States of America was founded on the principles "equality, civil rights, democracy, justice and freedom" for all people. As a result, the only way the colonies could justify the enslavement of African Americans was to depict them as less than human. Physical characteristics of skin color, nose width, eye shape, and hair texture became markers of racial identity. When Chinese and Japanese people came into the country in the nineteenth century, they were integrated into the status continuum somewhere between blacks and European whites. Along with privileging by racial identity came cultural hegemony, in which European culture was privileged above all other cultures. Africans and other racial groups were taught to have disdain for their native cultures and to revere European culture in all things. One area in which the influence of European cultural hegemony can be evidenced even today is in education. European literature, history, music, and visual arts are often still the standards against which all other cultural contributions are measured.

In order to understand the particulars of the ideology of race, one has only to read *Notes on the State of Virginia* by Thomas Jefferson. In his book, Jefferson writes a blueprint for racial stereotyping of African Americans that exists to this day.[2] According to Jefferson, the inferiority of African Americans started with the color of their skin, which is the foundation of a "greater or less share of beauty." Whites had "flowing hair and more elegant symmetry of form." He not only contended that African Americans were inferior in color, figure, and hair, but that they had a "very strong and disagreeable odor." Even the love African Americans displayed toward one another was inferior to that shared by whites, since black men were more prone to "desire" than "tender delicate mixture of sentiment and sensation." African Americans were "much inferior" to whites in reason, participating more in "sensation than reflection." Jefferson admitted that African Americans were more gifted than whites in music, having an "accurate ear for tune and time." However, he was not convinced that African Americans could equal whites in their ability to compose "extensive melodies" or "complicated harmony." At the end of the "Laws" section of his book, Jefferson wrote that the differences of "mental faculty and color" were "powerful obstacles to emancipation" of African Americans.

Brief History of Racially Segregated Worship

The ideology of race was not limited to the public square but was manifest in Christian worship. Though Africans worshiped in the same churches, they were often relegated to separate areas. One example is St. George's Methodist Church in Philadelphia in the eighteenth century. Though many white Methodists of that day objected to the practice of slavery, they did not believe that Africans were their equals.[3] As a result, the white members of St. George's built a gallery addition to the church and mandated that Africans worship there. Africans also felt stifled in their ability to express themselves in worship with verbal "Amens" or holy dancing. Since he and other African Americans were being oppressed and discriminated against, Richard Allen, a newly manumitted African slave, left St. George's and started the African Methodist Episcopal (A.M.E.) Church. The founding of the A.M.E. church was part of the black independent church movement that began as an expression of black resistance to white oppression after the Revolutionary War.[4] During the black independent church movement, many black Baptist churches were founded, as were new black denominations such as the African Methodist Episcopal Zion Church and the Colored Methodist Episcopal Church (now known as the Christian Methodist Episcopal Church).

The founding of black mainline Protestant churches was just the beginning of the black church movement. It began with African Americans coming out of white Baptist and Methodist churches because of racism. Then some African Americans came out of the black Baptist and black Methodist denominations because of a commitment to holiness.[5] In addition to a commitment to holiness, says Cheryl Sanders, the churches were countercultural in the sense that while African Americans in the Baptist and Methodist churches "assimilated and imitated the cultural and organizational models of European-American patriarchy," including styles of worship, the sanctified churches allowed African Americans to retain the traditions of oral music and ecstatic praise associated with slave religion.[6] The separation of African Americans and whites in Christian worship established a pattern of segregated worship that endures to this day.[7]

The Case for Segregated Worship

Martin Luther King Jr. argued that the church should cease its practice of segregated worship as a first step in its effort to achieve social reform. He made this statement even in the wake of tremendous social gains made by African Americans during the civil rights movement wherein black churches played a vital role. In black churches, civil rights workers heard prophetic and charismatic preaching that stirred their souls, comforted their spirits, and identified with the daily struggles they encountered. In those black churches, African Americans did not have to censor their speech to be politically correct or sensitive to the feelings of their white sisters and brothers. Black churches were spaces outside of their homes where they not only could speak their minds but where they also could hear messages of renewal to help them cope with the harsh realities of their lives throughout the coming week.

Many African Americans learn to appreciate black history in black churches, where they are taught about contributions to American history made by people such as Sojourner Truth, Mary McLeod Bethune, Marian Anderson, Frederick Douglass, Charles Drew, and Benjamin Banneker. Learning about other African Americans who were accomplished in so many ways inspires young people to make their own contributions.

Even in the twenty-first century, black churches are usually spaces where black people can be uncensored. They can hear sermons conceived with black life experiences in mind. They can hear music presented in genres that meet their spiritual needs. They can pray in ways they inherited from ancestors. They can be free to worship as long as they want. They can worship in an environment that is culturally affirming. They can be assured that their children will learn about their own black history in Sunday school or worship. As it relates to race, they can be accepted for who they are.

The Case for Truly Integrated Worship

Though the benefits of segregated worship are many, there are also benefits of integrated worship. Truly integrated worship is worship in which the many cultural practices of all races and ethnicities are valued and given space in the worship and life of the community.

Often worship that is deemed *multicultural* is simply an expression of dominant-culture hegemony in which the presence of people of various ethnicities and races is encouraged without allowing their cultural practices, traditions, and values (such as music, liturgy, preaching styles) to have a place in worship and community life. Churches that practice dominant-culture hegemony expect all members to conform to the ethos of the dominant culture, rather than allowing the dominant culture to be changed by the incorporation of other ways of being. Dominant-culture hegemony is akin to the melting-pot metaphor in which all ingredients are welcome but are expected to surrender their distinctiveness to assume the flavor and texture of the soup.[8] Truly integrated worship is akin to a salad in which all the ingredients blend to create wonderful flavors while each ingredient maintains its own distinctive taste, texture, and color.

Is it possible for a church to be truly integrated? Jin S. Kim, pastor of the Church of All Nations, a congregation of the Presbyterian Church (U.S.A.) in Minneapolis, not only believes it is possible but works with his congregation daily to make it a reality. In 2004, Kim, along with one hundred mostly Korean Americans, was granted a formal blessing by a larger congregation to found the Church of All Nations. The goal was to create a church wherein people from many different races and ethnic groups could come together as the body of Christ. Of the three hundred and fifty people who attend worship currently, 30 percent are Asian, 37 percent are white, 22 percent are black, and 10 percent are Latino/Latina. The congregation is truly living into its name by having people from more than twenty-five different nations represented, including Korea, Kenya, Sudan, Brazil, Japan, and the United States.

Elements of many different cultures are integrated into the English worship service held on Sundays at 10 a.m. Prayers are offered in many different languages. The Glorybound choir offers an extensive repertoire of songs and hymns that reflect the diversity of cultures. Fifty-six flags are displayed in the sanctuary to represent members' countries of origin and for which the congregation is in partnership or prayer. Testimony, a practice borrowed from the African American tradition in which individuals share their personal joys and struggles with the entire body, is a regular part of worship. Testimonies are sometimes given at offering time. On occasion, testimony replaces the sermon. At least twice a year, the entire service is devoted to testimony. While revealing personal experiences can be very risky, it can also serve as a conduit to understanding. When people hear each other's stories, they may begin to understand and experience the other in new ways.

On Sundays there is a Brazilian service conducted in Portuguese and a Sudanese service conducted in the Nuer language, as well as a service in French attended largely by West Africans—all attendees are full members of the

Church of All Nations. Each of these services has its own musical group. Though Kim would eventually like for the community to worship together in one service regularly (it does so now occasionally), he realizes that offering services in native languages brings tremendous comfort and a sense of belonging to new immigrants in the congregation. The leadership of the church reflects the diversity of the congregation, with pastors from Kenya, Togo, Brazil, China, Sudan, and the United States. With all the diversity that exists in the congregation, Kim contends that the greatest challenge is the black-white divide. In addition to being truly integrated as it relates to race and ethnicity, the church also dares to be counterimperial in that it rejects the capitalistic emphasis on production and material wealth as the symbols of identity, status, and success. At the Church of All Nations, the people who are held in highest esteem are those whose lives reflect faithfulness to God and care for one another.

Kim believes that the church thrives because its members are willing to engage in the hard conversations about white privilege and racism. They openly confess their complicity to unjust structures. Kim realizes that since he is Korean, it would be easy for the Korean culture to be the dominant culture. It would also be easy for white culture to be the dominant culture, since many people in the congregation are indoctrinated in it. However, he is intentional about reducing the influence of Korean and white cultures whenever possible to allow space for the many other cultures that exist. His congregation trusts him to be the "cultural referee."

Another congregation that embraces the salad metaphor is the Plymouth United Church of Christ in Oakland, California—also known as the "Jazz and Justice Church." The Plymouth congregation is 59 percent Euro-American, 31 percent African American, 5 percent Asian, and 5 percent

Latino. The jazz part of its identity is a metaphor in the sense that worship is a practice of living in the moment—a place where improvisation is welcome and there is no such thing as a mistake. Jazz is also experiential. Musicians from the Bay Area, many of whom are African American, provide music for the worship service throughout the year, which helps to create a lively and soulful worship environment. Though jazz is a large part of the church's identity, gospel music and hymns are also part of the musical repertoire.

Like the Church of All Nations, Plymouth UCC makes time in its worship service for testimony with a weekly spot known as "grace notes." The congregation strives to have open and honest discussions about racism, sexism, and ageism. As it relates to staff, they discovered a possible correlation between diversification of ministry staff and diversification of the congregation. For example, when a gay minister was hired, other lesbian, gay, bisexual, and transgendered (LGBT) people started to attend services. When a Cuban American minister was hired, other Latinas/Latinos began attending worship. The artwork in the church is African, Asian, or Latin American in origin; the church is intentional about not having white images of Jesus displayed. In addition, the church celebrates cultural festivals and holidays such as Juneteenth and Cinco de Mayo.

Conclusion

In response to the question "Do segregated churches imply racism?" we must respond with a resounding yes. The impetus for the establishment of segregated churches was racism embodied in censorship and the relegation of African Americans to separate spaces in white churches. Some believe that the antidote to traditional segregated church is the melting-pot church in which many different races and ethnicities are represented in body but are not represented in the leadership and must see their cultural practices and traditions subsumed into the dominant culture. This model is disingenuous at best. The real antidote to traditional segregated worship is the salad church. In the salad model, ethnic and racial groups are not required to deny or abdicate who they are to be part of the community. Their practices and traditions are welcomed and integrated into all aspects of worship and community life.

The perpetuation of segregated churches implies the ongoing need of various racial and ethnic groups to have spaces in which they can freely and unashamedly worship without fear of judgment or disdain—places where they can have a sense of pride and solidarity with people who look like them and who have similar values and shared experiences. Even in the twenty-first century, many racial and ethnic groups still have few public spaces in which their cultural practices and traditions are honored, respected, and embraced.

Therefore, the task for any church that seeks to be truly integrated is for church leaders to be willing to relinquish their power and then take it up again. The power that is relinquished is the *absolute* power that maintains a congregational ethos that is exclusive and discriminatory. The power taken up is a *shared* power that invites all people to the table, embraces who they are, and invites them to share their whole selves with the community. Shared power enables the church to become more like what it is meant to be: the body of Christ.

CHAPTER 9

POLICE BRUTALITY: UNDERSTANDING AND INTERVENING

The United States may well be experiencing another racial reckoning as a result of powerful resistance to the antiblack violence that has dominated the news since August 2014. The #BlackLivesMatter movement has been hailed by some as the next civil rights movement. The movement describes itself as a "decentralized network aiming to build the leadership and power of black people"[1] and has generated diverse protests, actions, and pressures for racial justice across the nation.

While #BlackLivesMatter did not begin in response to police brutality but with George Zimmerman's exoneration for killing Trayvon Martin, police brutality has been its central, galvanizing issue.[2] As a result, people of diverse racial identities who are committed to racial justice must engage and respond to police brutality in solidarity with the communities most targeted by police violence.

Social and Historical Context

Like many of more than one thousand people killed by police since August 2014, Michael Brown was unarmed.[3] He was black. He was shot by a white officer who was member of a department that was 95 percent white in a community whose residents are 70 percent African American.[4]

Brown's death was followed by widespread unrest in Ferguson, Missouri. Clashes between protestors and police brought images into homes across the nation of officers in riot gear; men, women, and children sprayed with tear gas; and tanks on the streets of a U.S. suburb. This, followed by the decision of a grand jury not to bring the officer to trial, sparked further resistance across the country and a national discussion about police violence against African Americans.

Meanwhile, public awareness of the frequency with which black men, women, and children die at the hands of police in the United States has continued to increase. Smartphone videos combined with social media's capacity to spread them have kept the public eye riveted on this reality of black life. As a result, white Americans have been forced to recognize that a crisis exists.

But the crisis itself is not new. In fact, the grief and rage that spilled out of Ferguson, and then New York, Baltimore, Cleveland, Chicago, and so many other places was the sort that erupts when a community is weary with first-hand experience of such tragedies. Direct, experiential knowledge that such tragedies keep repeating themselves erupts with a loud "Enough!"

Vigorous and organized resistance to police brutality is also not new. The first emergence of a black power movement came in response to fires and rebellion in Rochester, New York, in 1964. Black power activists critiqued the civil rights movement's focus on segregation as the major problem and insisted that the problem had more to do with resources, economics, jobs, and control over the media — in other words, all the things that convey power in social life.

What triggered the fires and mass resistance in Rochester? Police violence.

Fires and riots consumed Detroit in 1967 as well. Repeatedly asked to comment on the protestors' "violence," the iconic Rosa Parks refused to condemn them. Parks said that if the chokehold of white supremacy is so tight that this is the only form of resistance possible, then so be it. "It is better to protest than accept injustice," she said.[5] And like Rochester before it and Ferguson and Baltimore fifty years later, police brutality was the trigger for Detroit's fires.

If we do not already, those of us who want to be engaged in transformation for racial justice must understand the powerful force that police brutality has long exerted and continues to exert in and against communities of color daily. Beyond the most visible cases, persistent realities in the policing system create conditions not only in which violence against black communities becomes more likely, but in which the mere awareness that one might become a target creates corrosive and oppressive living conditions for African Americans.

What Is Police Brutality?

Police brutality is the phenomenon of police officers using force against a civilian beyond that which is required for handling a given situation.[6] Its most overt forms, of course, include the use of batons, pepper spray, Tasers, and, of course, guns.

But false arrests, unwarranted stops, and verbal abuse also constitute police brutality. For example, brutality commenced the moment a Seattle police officer began to berate an elderly black man who was using a golf club as a cane—despite the fact that she never hit him and that this happened long before she arrested him without justifiable cause.[7] Using one's policing power to threaten and coerce the very people one has sworn to serve is the most fundamental kind of moral distortion and abuse.

Those of us unfamiliar with the day-to-day realities of policing in black communities might be tempted to attribute the most egregious cases to the problem of a few bad apples, but police brutality exists as widespread, systemic sets of practices and policies. New York's stop-and-frisk policies, for example, which were in place for ten years before a federal judge ruled them unconstitutional, did not merely allow but actually encouraged officers to stop young people on the street simply for looking suspicious.[8] When white officers are already overrepresented in a police force heavily deployed in neighborhoods where most residents are not white, it's all but inevitable that "suspicious" will end up racialized.

That's precisely what Brooklyn resident Kasiem Walters describes in a powerful video interview. He conveys the impact of being stopped repeatedly for no reason as early as age 13, because he is black and lives in a neighborhood in which such is the normative policing practice. The high-schooler captures the emotional toll of such encounters when he says, "People shouldn't have to live in fear."[9] In listening to his interview, one cannot avoid the conclusion that at some point something is going to go awry. What happens when a grumpy, armed officer stops a young black man who has finally had enough because he's also had a bad day and simply cannot calmly tolerate being stopped one more time?

Such practices are themselves a form of brutality that creates a violent climate. Walters's *normal* experience is a state of high stress whenever he sees a police officer. He describes the internal panicked debate that ensues when he does. Should he stay on the same side of the street and risk being stopped or cross to the other side to avoid the officer and risk being seen as acting suspicious?

Another systemic dimension of brutality pertains to the unwillingness of the criminal justice system to hold police officers accountable when they do engage in excessive force. This too is a decades-old problem. Recall the four officers exonerated in the Rodney King case in Los Angeles in 1992. After that were many others, perhaps the most notable being the 1999 killing of Bronx resident Amadou Diallo in a hail of forty bullets. Despite the fact that Diallo was unarmed, not the suspect the officers were seeking, and (as autopsies suggested) had his hands up, all four officers were exonerated. New York City erupted in protest for months.

Increased calls have been made since Ferguson for the use of police body cameras, including by President Obama. Indeed, some data suggests that cameras might helpfully impact police behavior. But they are no panacea.[10] A video of Eric Garner's killing in Staten Island in July 2014 clearly shows Garner—who gave no indication of physical threat—gasping, "I can't breathe," eleven times while held in a chokehold banned by the NYPD.[11] But video footage notwithstanding, the grand jury decided there was not enough evidence, and all four officers walked away free men.

From stop-and-frisk practices, to FBI statistics that indicate blacks are killed by police every three to four days though unarmed 44 percent of the time,[12] to a justice system that refuses to hold officers accountable, police brutality is not a problem of a few bad officers. This nation is contending with a deeply layered and longstanding social crisis. Responses therefore need to be equally layered and multi-directed, and sustained pressure is critical for keeping alive the public will to demand that it stop.

How Does This Happen?

How is it possible that in a nation now fifty years past the civil rights movement, African Americans who encounter police, whatever the reason, are three times more likely to end up dead than are white Americans?[13] (It's critical to remember here how often African Americans are confronted by police for reasons that come nowhere near breaking the law.) Several factors offer at least a partial response to this question.

First, police officers hold significant discretionary power. This is partly a result of discretionary power being conferred upon them by the Supreme Court in increasing measure over the last four decades. Michelle Alexander's book *The New Jim Crow* provides a stunning analysis of a series of cases in which citizens tried to hold police officers accountable for racially biased profiling while the Court repeatedly ruled that the only way to prove racially discriminatory practice and policy—and thus the only way to stop a practice for being unconstitutional—was to prove racist intent.[14] Few will openly admit to intending racism; thus, this is an impossibly high legal bar that has allowed racist behavior to continue to run rampant.

Another layer of discretion has to do with the social power conferred on police. Anyone who has been pulled over for speeding is likely to know the nervous feeling that can result. Imagine an officer behaving in a rude or aggressive manner during such a stop. All else being equal (no racial, age, or gender difference), it takes a high level of confidence and courage to challenge such treatment in this most mundane level of encounter. Combine this ethos with the reality that most complaints pit an officer's word against a civilian's, and one can easily see that power functions to give police a great deal of leeway in terms of how they treat people.

Police officers may be no more likely to abuse power in the face of such discretion than any nonuniformed civilian might be. However, they do not need to be more likely to do so in order for such discretion to create a policing crisis. For the shocking evidence revealed about human behavior in the infamous Stanford experiment suggests that many people will abuse power if given the opportunity. When two groups of people were set up randomly to be prison guards and prisoners during this 1971 experiment, within a few days the guards—seemingly average, normal people—became so brutal in their treatment of the prisoners that the experiment had to be halted.[15] The experiment strongly indicates that any of us are at risk of abusing power. When those in such a position have weapons and are backed by a system that has repeatedly shown it will confer the benefit of the doubt against civilians, it is no surprise we have a crisis.

An added layer to the crisis is the persistence of racial bias. Alexander cites a study that demonstrates the extent to which antiblack racial bias is a pervasive and normal part of Americans' attitudes even among those who disavow racist beliefs. Racism is in the air as a result of U.S. history, social organization, images in media, and a host of other factors. Most of us do not even realize the extent to which we harbor biases.[16] Social psychology is increasingly finding that our racial socialization is so deep that work to undo these biases (diversity trainings, multicultural appreciation, etc.) is extremely limited in its efficacy unless it is rigorous, consistent, and ongoing.[17]

Meanwhile, as with discretionary power, there is no reason to expect a police officer to be any less likely to be shaped by, and thus act out of, racial bias. Saying so is not a defense of brutality. It is an honest recognition of the depth of the problem and another argument for seeing such violence as systemic and, thus, requiring unrelenting and multi-directed responses. Anything less becomes a willingness to tolerate police violence against communities of color.

Racial Differences Matter

The depth of racial separation in the United States makes police violence much more difficult to stop. This is because it has been hard to convince the demographic majority of the population (i.e., whites) that there is a problem at all. After Michael Brown was killed, stark racial differences were apparent on everything from whether race was a significant factor in his death to whether the officer should be tried for murder.[18] Eighty percent of blacks (compared to 18 percent of whites) said that the killing "raises important issues about race that merit discussion."[19]

White people know very little about the day-to-day experience of African Americans because most white people know almost no African Americans in a meaningful way. A 2013 poll indicated that most white Americans have a social network that is 91 percent white. Three-quarters reported that "the network of people with whom they discuss important matters is entirely white."[20] This level of racial separation makes it difficult for whites to accept what they hear their fellow citizens saying about police violence. Meanwhile, if one has never been stopped because of one's skin tone and has primarily had positive experiences with police, one is repeatedly confirmed in the false belief that all officers are basically trustworthy and the law is objective and just.

Another racially inflected response exists in public debate over the legitimacy of the "violence" of protestors in Ferguson and, later, in Baltimore. Here again, when one expects and experiences a system responsive to oneself, one is more likely to presume "legal" and "legitimate" protests to be the only morally acceptable options. Those whose experience is with a system that has never yet been responsive—as was the case with Rosa Parks—know something very different about what is legitimate, even required, to even be heard.

The point here is not to slip into a simplistic debate over whether or not violence in protests is legitimate. It is to emphasize that larger systems of racial division ensure that whites are insulated from the realities African Americans contend with every day. These exacerbate our racial divisions and must be taken into account if we care about justice and wish to respond to police brutality.

Responding to Police Brutality

The depth with which our experiences and perceptions of police brutality are racially inflected, and the many layers that create this crisis, make it urgent that we listen and respond to what #BlackLivesMatter has to say and the ways it is directing collective energy for justice. This crisis will not be easily solved, and we should all be wary of simple or quick solutions. Yet we can and must choose to act and press to find constructive ways to intervene nonetheless. The kinds of interventions demanded range from critical protest to constructive advocacy. Whatever the form, connecting with others who are (and have long been) active in doing so is critical to sustaining the hope and will power to continue doing so in the face of a seemingly intractable problem.

At the most basic level, justice-committed people must be part of the protests and rallies being held in so many communities across the country. Rallies do not alone necessarily lead to immediate policy changes—although a myriad of long-needed and real changes have been made in Missouri because of the Ferguson protests.[21] But protest does generate and sustain critical visibility that keeps the crisis in the public eye. Such visibility creates a kind of persistent, productive pressure on policy makers. It also sends police departments the message that the public is watching and will not wait quietly until the next visible, egregious case of violence transpires.

Community policing is on a different end of the intervention continuum and is another way to advocate in local environments. The philosophy of community policing presumes, for example, that "citizens are most likely to respond positively to law enforcement efforts that mesh with their own concerns."[22] This is a shift away from officers seeing themselves exclusively as law enforcers—in which case, according to former Madison, Wisconsin, police chief David C. Couper, police focus all their efforts on watching for violations of the law. When Couper was chief, for example, he assigned officers long term to certain neighborhoods and charged them to "work with community members to choose which crimes to prioritize."[23] This was a different way of giving officers discretion.

Arguments for community policing increased after Ferguson. Indeed, a survey of Madison residents conducted in 2013 revealed an "above-average level of trust in law enforcement and a high degree of two-way interaction between police and citizens."[24] Similar transformations have happened in Los Angeles. Between 2002 and 2009, the police chief made racial tensions a priority for the LAPD, which altered its policing practices. As a result,

African American and Latino/a voter approval of the police increased by double digits.[25]

But no one approach should be seen as the answer. A series of police killings of unarmed black citizens in Madison in recent years has reminded advocates of community policing (both within and outside the police department) how difficult it is to create and sustain real change.

Conclusion

Those who advocate for justice need not and should not focus on one set of practices or agree about every single strategy. What is essential is that those who believe in justice act, with others and in sustained ways, in response to some of the causes outlined here. Many others could be named.

Moreover, it's critical (and energizing) to know that the conditions leading to police violence are not only receiving attention at a national level, but—like #BlackLivesMatter itself—are also meaningfully addressed and challenged at the local level, in active coalitions across racial lines, to potentially transformative effects.

It is no overstatement to insist that this nation is in a watershed moment. Public attention has made it all but impossible for anyone to ignore the crisis of police brutality against black and brown communities in the United States. The question is this: On which side of history will we each choose to stand?

PART III

WHAT TO DO

CHAPTER 10

WHITENESS AND WHAT
WHITE PEOPLE CAN DO

Many white people rightly argue that *we* did not commit genocide against native peoples in this country.* *We* didn't personally enslave African Americans. *We* didn't fight in the war that stole half of Mexico and that is now the western United States. *We* weren't even alive when the Chinese Exclusion Act happened, and *we* didn't intern Japanese citizens during World War II. Those things happened decades, centuries ago. So why should white people today bear any responsibility for something that *we* didn't do?

The simple answer is that white people continue to benefit today from a system that was built and still operates to give us an unfair advantage and others an unfair disadvantage. It is true that many white people are struggling to make ends meet and don't feel very privileged when

*This chapter is written by white people to other white people specifically. For that reason, "we" refers to white people. Others certainly are encouraged to read this and participate in the discussion.

credit cards are maxed out and budgets stretched to the limits. Nevertheless, if we think *we* have it bad, others have it much worse. And if we truly believe that all children of God are equal, we need to act when some are not treated as equally as others.

One sign of white advantage or white privilege is that we don't actually *have* to do anything. It is tempting to shrug our shoulders and excuse our inaction on lack of political leadership, complexity of the issues, and mixed messages about just what to do. This chapter explains whiteness as a concept that arose in order to separate and give privilege to one group of people, explains what white privilege is with some examples, and offers some ideas about how to help dismantle racism.

The Origins of Whiteness in America

In the book *Dear White Christians*, author Jennifer Harvey explains the history of whiteness as a racial category in the United States and how it arose as an identity simultaneous with and related to the "violent and complete subjugation of the darker skinned."[1] Following is a simplified summary of how race first emerged in the United States.

Despite the popular narrative about America's founders coming to escape religious persecution, Christopher Columbus sailed the ocean blue in 1492 looking for treasure. Most Europeans who settled in the Virginia area were English elites coming to pursue wealth. Tobacco was the most lucrative crop, and it required large numbers of workers to produce. While the primary source of labor was originally tenant farmers from Europe, this quickly transformed to an indentured servant system, which was more profitable for the colonial elites. Harvey points out that, hard as indentured servanthood was, it never approached the level and cruelty of chattel slavery.[2]

The first documentation of an African servant in America was in 1619. There is not much written about the period from 1619 to 1640, but a court case in 1640 changed everything. Three indentured servants escaped from their owner and were caught. One was a Dutchman, one a Scotchman, and one a person of African descent. The two Europeans were given whippings and sentenced to additional time as servants. But the African, also whipped, was sentenced to return and to serve his master for life. No European servant ever received this sort of life sentence.

Harvey observes that the other notable element in the case was that for the first time, "physical difference was invoked specifically and clearly as a means to assign a radically different servitude status to an African person vis-à-vis his European counterparts."[3] The African was called a "Negro" in the court case, referring to his dark skin color (*negro* in Spanish means "dark" or "black").

At the same time, the term used by the English to refer to themselves had evolved from "Christian" (separating themselves from "savage" native peoples and "heathen" Africans), to "English" and "free." But by the end of the century, with the ongoing, brutal genocide of Native Americans and chattel slavery for forcibly relocated Africans, a new term emerged for the elite: white.

This short history explains what people mean when they say that race is a social construct. It was created by people in power based on physical traits such as skin color, hair texture, and eye color to lump people from different ethnic cultures into a group in order to control them.

Not surprisingly, over the next centuries, other lighter skinned people coming to the United States were willing to participate in this system based on skin color in order to reap the benefits that came with compliance. So just as native peoples from dozens of different ethnic groups and languages were lumped together as *Indians* in this white supremacy model, so darker skinned Africans from many different ethnic groups and languages were bunched together as *Negro* slaves. And lighter skinned peoples lost their particular ethnic identities for the most part in exchange for becoming *white*. Is it any wonder most white people wonder what their heritage is? We may be proud that our great-grandparents were German or Italian and spoke their native languages at home. Yet we also know that if they were light skinned, they (or their children) soon relinquished many of their ethnic customs in order to pass for white and enjoy the privileges that came with that status. Is it any wonder that, while not knowing the entire racist history of the country, most white people feel uncomfortable talking about racism? It's often called *white shame*. Harvey writes:

> Although a majority of whites on this land base were not slaveholders themselves, all occupied Native land, and most refused to disrupt the institution of slavery. Even those whose economic interests were harmed by the existence of slavery benefited from it in various ways. Moreover, slavery could not have functioned were not most whites — rich or poor, third generation or new immigrant — willing to allow it to continue. As long as the system could rely on light-skinned people to choose not to be a safe haven when African peoples ran away, and to choose to serve as overseers, to mill the cotton that moved from South to North, to rely on wages earned in that production to feed their families, and on a myriad of other similar behaviors that ensured slavery functioned, it did not matter that most whites did not themselves own slaves.[4]

Of course, not only did native peoples and forcibly relocated Africans suffer under this system based on skin color. All people in the country who could not fit under the white umbrella have experienced discrimination. And resistance and rebellion have been a constant reaction by darker skinned peoples and are part of our national history absent in many school history textbooks. In addition, many white people, including many Christians, have given their lives in the struggle against a racist system based on inequality and violence.

White Supremacy Continued

Most people passing for white through the nation's history have not consciously participated in this white supremacist system built on the backs of the forced and underpaid labor of darker skinned peoples. Yet the inequalities did not end with the Civil War or even the Civil Rights Acts of 1964 and 1968. The common narrative is that the Civil War ended slavery in the South. Yet we know that is not true. Policies were continually enacted by white political leaders that kept non-whites poor and with fewer resources. Following is just one example:

> The federal government, starting in the 1930s, demolished many integrated neighborhoods and built segregated public housing, separate projects for blacks and separate projects for whites so it created segregation where none had existed before. The second major policy was the federal housing administration, starting in the late 1930s, began to insure loans to mass production builders to build subdivision suburbs around the country so that whites could move from urban areas to the suburbs and the federal housing administration guaranteed these loans to mass production builders on the explicit condition that no homes be sold to African Americans.[5]

Massive investments went into creating segregated housing. And unlike other forms of discrimination, when you change the landscape and infrastructure, you cannot undo that simply by ceasing to do that which you did before. . . . So if you have massively invested in the creation of white suburbs through the interstate highway system and through providing the kinds of loans and tax breaks to the creation of all white suburbs, you cannot undo the damage of that simply by no longer making those investments.[6]

White Privilege Today

The term *white privilege* is used to refer to the unearned advantages enjoyed by white people in the United States. Perhaps these privileges are not as visible as they once were. One does not walk past slave pens and watch forcibly removed Africans being sold to white masters. We don't have separate drinking fountains for whites. Yet whether we feel privileged or not, those of us who are white still benefit from the present social order of this society. And as a growing movement is pointing out, racial injustices are visible if we only pay attention. For example, the increased instances (or the increased attention and visibility) of police shootings of innocent black men and children are evidence of an institution that historically protected white supremacist interests and was never reformed.

Many white folk would prefer to ignore or deny this reality; this is one of the reasons that racism is often defined in terms of personal prejudice. It is easier to think of racism and the tensions and inequality around issues of race as a particular kind of prejudice. That allows certain white people to say that since we are not prejudiced, we don't need to worry about racism or concern ourselves with working toward dismantling it.

Examples of White Privilege

Whites can move into an apartment or house wherever they want and assume that their neighbors will be friendly, oblivious, or unconcerned.

Whites can walk into any store and not fear being followed by security guards or watched.

Whites can dress like slobs and not feel judged for having an attire that shows they are obviously poor or lazy. On dress-down Friday, they can really dress down.

Whites aren't afraid of the police. They consider them their friends. Likewise, whites can call 911 about a fire or for an ambulance and trust that help will come immediately.

Whites can contact any doctor, lawyer, electrician, or plumber and assume they will be treated well.

Whites can check into any hotel and not worry about being told there is no vacancy or being placed in a substandard room while being charged the highest price.

Whites may be alarmed when pulled over for a traffic violation, but they assume they will just get a ticket and not be harassed, searched, or arrested.

If they receive bad service at a business, whites can confront the clerk and insist on seeing the manager while not fearing harassment by the manager or arrest.

If white people fail, their race or moral character is not questioned.

A group of white men armed with assault rifles and other guns can walk into a multiracial crowd of angry protestors in Ferguson, Missouri, and not be shot by police.

Yet racism is a system, not a prejudice. White people and people of color—African Americans, Latinos/Latinas, Asian Americans, Native Americans—have very different experiences in the United States because of this system of privilege based on skin color. This may make white people feel uncomfortable, but it is a fact.

Every year, the National Urban League publishes the Equality Index, which compares the conditions of black, Latino, and white Americans using a comprehensive set of variables, including health, education, economics, social justice, and civic engagement. The beginning point is a line from the original Constitution of the United States that counted African Americans as three-fifths of a person for purposes of taxation and state representation—or 0.60, using whites as the standard 1.0. (The Constitution was corrected by the 13th Amendment in 1865.) When the index is lower than 1.0, it indicates that black or Latino Americans are not doing as well as whites in the area being measured. For 2015, the index was 0.72 for blacks and 0.78 for Latinos, essentially unchanged from previous years.[7]

There is a wealth of information in this index. For example, black Americans are at 0.80 and Latinos are at 1.07 relative to white Americans with regard to health. These numbers have improved greatly in the short time since the Affordable Care Act was enacted (i.e., Obamacare). Yet in the economic category, the index stands at 0.56 for blacks and 0.61 for Latinos.

In *The Hidden Cost of Being African American*, Thomas Shapiro explains that the true disparity in the economic well-being between black and white Americans is not found primarily in the fact that the average black family earns sixty-four cents for every dollar earned by the average white family. Rather, it has to do with the way that wealth is passed from generation to generation; the net worth of the average white family is $81,000, compared to

$8,000 for the average black family. The traditional argument is that the difference in wealth has to do with disparities in education, job, and income, but when middle class families with equivalent education, jobs, and incomes are compared, the average black family still owns only twenty-six cents for every dollar owned by its white counterpart.[8]

In a system that gives unfair economic advantages to whites, it is difficult for people of color to build wealth. One argument for reparations for people harmed by this system is to help them catch up and to enable them to help future generations succeed. For example, one of the harshest, long-term outcomes of the 1921 Tulsa race massacre—in which whites destroyed a large business and housing community of middle class, prosperous black people and murdered over three hundred innocent men, women, and children—was the destruction of accumulated wealth that was slowly being passed from one generation to the next, allowing children to attend college and move up the economic ladder. Reparations were never granted. In fact, the Oklahoma legislature passed a law the year following the massacre (still called a "riot" by most of the media) that no reparations could ever be requested. In September 2015, some ninety-five years after the fact, the Tulsa police chief issued an apology for the failure to protect black people. Yet demands for reparations in the form of college tuition and loan assistance are still denied, making the confession rather empty.

Whiteness and Youth Today

For a 2015 MTV documentary *White People*, Pulitzer Prize–winning journalist and filmmaker Jose Antonio Vargas led some uncomfortable discussions with a diverse group of young adults from across the country about whiteness.[9]

He encouraged them to be brutally honest. One of the first questions he asked was "What is white?" Answers included, "It's the default," "It's the norm," It's the good thing." When he asked how white people felt talking with people of another race, answers included, "I feel totally comfortable" and "I could care less about someone's race; I was never taught to notice it." Almost all young white Americans he interviewed consider themselves color-blind. He reported that three out of four young white Americans say that society would be better off if we never acknowledged race. Four out of five young white Americans say they feel uncomfortable discussing race issues. Yet others, especially people of color, said that having this point of view was dismissive of people of color. To not acknowledge racism experienced by non-white people ignores the reality in which they live. Most white kids report never talking about racism with their parents. If we think racism will disappear naturally with the future generations, this documentary exposes the error of our thinking. White people need to understand how racism works, and they need to work to end it. It will not end by itself, as recent events in our country attest.

What to Do About White Privilege

Our country has never had a conversation about what to do with such a large group of people who have been forcefully placed at the margins and how to help them. Joseph Darby, former pastor of Morris Brown A.M.E. Church in Charleston, South Carolina, said this after the 2015 killing of nine black church members by a young white racist: "All this 'kumbaya stuff' will be meaningless without combating the institutional racism that still defines the state 'and the state of the union': underfunded, segregated schools, neglected black towns, unjust voter I.D. laws, gentrification and joblessness in the cities, outsized rates of African-Americans in prison."[10]

Of course, when we talk about racism in this country, we are not only talking about whites and blacks, as Robette Ann Dias explains:

> If we only understand race as being Black or White, and we only have a framework for understanding racism as dynamics between Black people and White people, defining the "race problem" as the legacy caused by African enslavement, then the solutions we can imagine are constrained to rectifying that dynamic. In the real world, this means we could solve the problem of civil rights, full inclusion, and control of resources for African-Americans, we could even make reparations but still not have touched American Indian's[sic] racial justice struggle to reclaim land and sovereignty. Nor would we have solved any issues around immigration and civil rights for people from (or whose ancestors were from) parts of the world that the US restricts legal immigration like Latin and South America, Africa, Asia and the Middle East. The homelands of Puerto Rico, Hawai'i, Alaska, and Guam would still not be returned to their people. And our economy would continue to depend on neo-colonial practices around the world.[11]

Unfortunately, in a racist society where skin color makes such a difference, one cannot simply opt out. People of color certainly cannot ignore the rules of the system. White people can ignore their advantage, but it undeniably exists. Ignoring privilege is itself a sign of privilege.

One natural response of white people is to feel shame. If you are white and someone were to ask you what makes you most proud about your race, you probably would feel uneasy. At a gut level, we know something is wrong and don't really know what it means to be white. We watch white racists with horror as they claim superiority for whiteness. We know that's wrong, but just who are we? Feeling some shame for participating in a system we didn't create but that privileges us is healthy to a degree. Yet we cannot be immobilized by this shame. Instead, we can recognize it and work to dismantle the system.

Another common response to deal with our uneasiness is to seek friendships with people of color. It is certainly good to develop long-term, deep friendships with people from different ethnic cultures, but this does not replace the need to advocate and work for dismantling the systemic racism that affects entire groups of people.

Unfortunately, there is no blueprint offered here. It will take more than individual responses to eradicate racism in this country and repair damaged, broken communities, but individual responses are important. Following are some examples.

Live with the discomfort racism creates. Resist the urge to ignore or reason away the bad feelings that come with realizing that you are privileged and cannot fix the problem alone. While not allowing these feelings to consume you, let them be a spiritual source of motivation to keep active in the fight against racism.

Do not deny the advantages you have, but make a lifetime commitment to end racism. White people don't have to be rich to receive privilege or advantages. You may have grown up poor as a white person. But if you are white and went to public school as a child, chances are that your school received better resources and teachers than the schools in neighborhoods where people of color lived. In addition, you were less likely to be detained, suspended, and expelled for school infractions than people of color were. If you own a home, chances are that you had no problem securing a loan, perhaps even a government loan to get started, and that the value of your property is going up, unlike the value of homes where people of color live. Their neighborhoods are often close to industrial sites and hazardous waste zones. These are generalizations, but if they ring true for you, let them be an added incentive to work to change the system. Consider using more of your resources for this cause.

Listen to what non-white groups are saying and demanding. Take advantage of the current public conversation about racism and what people of color suggest as remedies. The Black Lives Matter movement is one popular group that is offering concrete demands. Many public radio and television programs are focusing on what needs to be done to dismantle racism.

Question what you have been taught about other races and are passing on to others, perhaps unconsciously. Otis Moss III explains that prior to the end of the Civil War, black people were viewed as less than fully human but were not feared for the most part. After the Civil War, a concerted effort was made to teach white people to fear all people of color, especially men, so that they would not compete with white laborers.[12] Today, one needs to watch only a few minutes of the local news to see image after image of mostly people of color getting arrested. This has the effect of maintaining a level of fear in the population of people of color. People of color are engaged in many more positive things than robbing others. Many people of color report instances of white people crossing to the other side of the street or clutching their child's hand when a person of color approaches. Challenge assumptions and think about what you are teaching children about how to interact with people from other backgrounds. They should not be feared any more than white people.

As a Middle Eastern man, Jesus himself likely had dark skin. God is not white either. The Divine is a mystery in whose image all colors of people are made. Challenge places where Jesus and God are portrayed as light-skinned white men, including Sunday school rooms.

Speak up. White people can challenge others when they observe racism. If you regularly observe a security guard following people of color in a store, ask the guard why he or she is only following people of color. If you are afraid of confrontation, report the guard to the manager. If you see police yelling at or roughing up a person of color, make your presence known. If you have a camera, record the situation. It is your right. Some police departments have added body cameras to their officers' uniforms, but until there is a nationwide retraining of police, it is important to have as many eyes as possible on an institution that historically has unjustly harmed people of color.

Show up. When instances of racial violence occur, there are often vigils and protests. The presence of white people is important for showing people of color that it is not *their* problem and that white people are concerned. Showing Up for Racial Justice (SURJ) is a national organization helping organize white people for racial justice. Check out its Web site (http://www.showingupforracialjustice.org), and see what local groups are participating. Often you can get on a list and be notified when there are events to attend.

Educate yourself. There are no experts on white privilege and racism. It is a lifelong journey, and much more focus is being given to the role white people can play in changing the system. Join or form a reading group to read books together to strengthen your actions. Here are some books to consider:

> *Dear White Christians: For Those Still Longing for Racial Reconciliation* by Jennifer Harvey
> *The New Jim Crow: Mass Incarceration in the Age of Colorblindness* by Michelle Alexander

Slavery by Another Name: The Re-Enslavement of Black Americans from the Civil War to World War II by Douglas A. Blackmon

Yellow: Race in America beyond Black and White by Frank Wu

Blood Done Sign My Name by Timothy Tyson

Privilege, Power, and Difference by Allan Johnson

Privilege: A Reader edited by Michael S. Kimmel and Abby L. Ferber

White Privilege: Essential Readings on the Other Side of Racism by Paul Rothenberg

Explaining White Privilege to a Broke White Person by Gina Crosley-Corcoran

Between the World and Me by Ta-Nehisi Coates

The Half Has Never Been Told: Slavery and the Making of American Capitalism by Edward E. Baptist

After the June 17, 2015, massacre of nine black church members in Charleston, South Carolina, much attention was given to taking down the Confederate flag at the state capitol. In addition, many called not only for taking down some of the statues of white leaders in the capitol who owned and promoted slavery, but also replacing them with statues of people of color who have contributed to the state's wealth. Look into the white heroes lifted up in your state or city, and find out the history of racism there and what contributions have been made by people of color that have not been given fair recognition.

Is there a museum near you that tells the true story of the genocide, broken treaties, and forced relocation of Native Americans, the enslavement of Africans, the Underground Railroad, the internment of Japanese Americans during World War II, or the history of immigrants in your area? Is there a museum nearby that provides information about how part of Mexico was stolen and its citizens became undocumented and unwanted? If so, patronize that museum. Many Jews have funded impressive Holocaust museums around the world. Why are there not more museums in the United States that tell the real story of the effects of racism on people of color? Attend a White Privilege Conference (http://www.whiteprivilegeconference.com), where you can learn more about white privilege, find out how to combat racism, and network with others.

Give money. Many communities of color in this country suffer from generations of brokenness. Search for groups who are making efforts to transform the people in these communities. For example, give to racial ethnic colleges or scholarship programs in your area that focus on disadvantaged kids and help them overcome obstacles.

Conclusion

It is tempting to be overwhelmed and not know where to begin or what to say. The Bible is filled with examples of people who feel unqualified and inadequate to speak. For instance, Jeremiah was a very hesitant prophet, and Jesus' disciples stumbled all over themselves. The Bible also has examples of people with privilege, such as Moses, who stepped up. Moses passed for Egyptian and was safe in Pharaoh's court. But when he witnessed racial injustice, he was compelled to act, despite having no idea of what to say. While white people are not being asked to lead the movement for racial justice, we are in a place where we can challenge unfair advantage and be more active participants in righting the wrongs that harm so many.

CHAPTER 11

THE CHURCH'S RESPONSE

The immediate question when discussing the church's response to racism is, of course, *which* church? Since Jesus assembled the first motley crew of disciples, the community gathered has been anything but a homogenous group of saints. Churches have always been a mixed bag of those who attempt to follow the good news and those who use and twist the message for selfish gain.

European settlers who brought their religion with them to America were no exception. They did not discover anything except a land they had not known existed, filled with people they did not know. Land was mostly stolen and native inhabitants were forcibly removed. Those displaced did not leave their homes peacefully but resisted. The European settlers—some religious, many not—banded together and formed militias and armies to make room for their "city on a hill," which led to the slaughter of American innocents, the original sin of this country that has yet to be confessed and repaired.

For the most part, church leaders blessed this genocide on religious grounds. Leaders would later argue for the inferiority of non-white races and justify the enslavement of Africans, the criminalization of intermarriage, and the countless invasions of other lands, often distorting biblical texts to legitimize their actions and bless injustice.

Not all European Christians in America agreed with the white supremacist system established by the new colonial government. Many white Christians risked their lives to object and protect. But they were the exceptions to the rule. Most Christian churches endorsed racist government policies, which was no surprise, since the government leaders arose from the rank-and-file membership of these same churches.

We also must acknowledge the response of enslaved Africans who were taught biblical stories from their masters and heard words of freedom, justice, and equality. It is no surprise that the Africans rebelled.

> Since we landed on these shores in 1619, and our toes touched the red clay of Georgia and South Carolina, we have been fighting. Three hundred slave insurrections have been recorded in history, and only three of them did not occur in church. Any time people of color got together and we started worshiping our God, we knew that our God did not intend for us to be in bondage. We were fighting from the moment that we arrived here.[1]

So today, in a country where even Confederate flag–waving, KKK card–carrying, proud racists identify themselves as Christian, we need to clarify just which church we are talking about when we discuss the church's response to racism in a post-Obama era. For our purposes, we are talking mostly about member churches of the National Council of Churches, sometimes called historic or mainline churches. We are talking about churches that, at least for the last quarter of a century, have spoken out in favor of racial justice. Most of these historic, institutional bodies have evolved, participated, and benefited from the racist past and say they want to reckon with it. We will first examine what it means to reconcile and then look at some recent attempts of churches to confront racial injustice.

No Justice, No Reconciliation

Toward the end of his life, Martin Luther King Jr. and other civil rights leaders were increasingly frustrated with the white churches that said they supported the movement for racial justice. When King began his public advocacy work, he was working not for racial integration but for racial justice. Separate but equal was the law of the land, and his efforts were focused not on changing the "separate" part of the law (segregation) but rather the "equal" part. Black bus drivers should be hired to drive in the black parts of town. If whites could sit in unoccupied black sections of buses, blacks should be able to sit in unoccupied white sections. King accepted separateness as long as there was equality.

As courageous white Christians and students showed up to support the struggle for justice, however, King was impressed. He soon had a vision of a future beloved community where all would live together in racial harmony. White Christians loved this vision of a beloved community, yet they proved themselves too willing to back away from the ugly fight against racial injustice in order to jump to the kumbaya moment where Christians of all colors would link arms and be one. King insisted that the beloved community could only come about when justice had been done—not before.

Still today, many people of color distrust white-led churches because nothing has been done to fix centuries of racist violence and destruction of communities. Calls and demands for reparations for broken, damaged communities have largely been ignored or downplayed. White-led churches are willing to put energy behind cultural-competency classes so that people can appreciate ethnic differences. We love diverse worship services because they make us look like some beloved community. But people of color ask, "Whose needs are being met? Is this simply meeting the needs of white leaders who are uncomfortable with white privilege and separateness and who want to feel better by sweeping the dirty racial sin under a rug rather than dealing with it?

Getting to racial reconciliation cannot skip the step of doing justice to communities of color and changing the institutional racism in this country. True reconciliation goes something like this: If a person has been violated, the violator does not get to declare forgiveness and reconciliation before righting the wrong. The role of the violator is to confess what has been done, apologize to the victim, and repair the wrong.

At that point, once justice has been accomplished, it is for the victim to decide whether or not to forgive and whether or not to reconcile with the oppressor. The victim may never wish to reconcile, and the perpetrator must accept that. Sadly, most churches led by white leaders still today want to focus on the beloved community when justice has never been served.

Many white churches concerned about racial justice today feel uncomfortable that Sunday is still the most segregated hour in the week in America. One response is to fix that discomfort by working harder to make people of color feel welcome in white churches. Better yet, white people could join churches led by people of color and learn to follow non-white leaders. But perhaps a mostly white church can still do much for racial justice by working with and being led by people of color who may or may not wish to worship with them.

Attempts at Racial Justice

The rest of this chapter offers examples of Christians responding to racial injustice in a variety of ways. Each example is followed by some questions for discussion. Don't let these examples discourage you, but use them to challenge your group to evaluate what you are doing and to urge you onward.

The Black Manifesto

On a Sunday morning in May 1969, James Forman, backed by a large organization of black leaders, interrupted worship at Riverside Church in New York City and read aloud a manifesto to a startled crowd of worshipers. This document included the following:

> Racist white America has exploited our resources, our minds, our bodies, our labor. . . . We are demanding $500,000,000 from the Christian white churches and the Jewish synagogues. This . . . is not a large sum of money, and we know that the churches and synagogues have a tremendous wealth and its membership, white America, has profited and still exploits black people. We are also not unaware that the exploitation of colored peoples around the world is aided and abetted by the white Christian churches and synagogues. . . . Fifteen dollars for every black brother and sister in the United States is only a beginning of the reparations due us as people who have been exploited and degraded, brutalized, killed and persecuted.[2]

The "Black Manifesto" mentioned using that money to fund a Southern land bank, publishing and printing industries, audiovisual networks, a research skills center, a training center, assistance to the National Welfare Rights Organization, a National Black Labor and Defense Fund, and the establishment of an International Black Appeal to raise money for cooperative businesses in the United States and the African motherland and for a black university in the South. The leaders of the movement wanted the money in order help black communities move forward.

The responses were mixed among the mainline denominations, most of which were visited personally by the group of black leaders. Not surprisingly, some shut their doors entirely to the group, some defended what they already were doing to help disadvantaged groups of people, and some initiated new programs in response to the manifesto, although they insisted on managing these programs and the funding themselves. Only one denomination gave some money to the Black Economic Development Conference, the organization run by the black leaders.

Communities of color have made a number of concrete demands for reparations or land returns throughout the centuries. Calls for reparations usually insist on a long-term effort over several generations in order to effect lasting change on the economic and political lives of those affected by racism. They often fall on deaf ears or are rejected immediately by white-led institutions.

How did your church's leaders respond to the Black Manifesto?
What financial resources does your church give to organizations led by people of color to address needs they have defined?
How would you respond to a modern manifesto by people of color?

Denominational Calls for Racial Justice and Reparations

Since 2000, the Episcopal Church, the Presbyterian Church (U.S.A.), the United Methodist Church, the United Church of Christ, and the Unitarian Universalist Association have all passed resolutions calling for studies of the history of racial injustice, their complicity in it, and the possibility of reparations. Many denominations have created resources to help local congregations engage in study and reflection from their local context. Noteworthy are the United Church of Christ's program "Sacred Conversation on Race," which offers resources for local congregations and encourages a host of actions.[3] The Episcopal Church does not have a curriculum, but it does have an antiracism training manual, *Seeing the Face of God in Each Other*, which emphasizes white privilege and the need for justice.[4]

Perhaps the Episcopal Church is the furthest along in terms of calling for confession about slavery on a local and national level. It has passed a number of resolutions on racism and reparations, one in 2006 that urged "the Church at every level to call upon Congress and the American people to support legislation initiating study of and dialogue about the history and legacy of slavery in the United States and the proposals for monetary and non-monetary reparations to the descendants of the victims of slavery.[5] Another resolution passed the same year apologized and repented for the church's participation in slavery and directed every diocese to collect detailed information about how its churches had benefited from slavery.[6] While most churches have not followed through, some impressive accounts have been made by churches built by slave labor. In addition, some public confessions have been made.[7]

The Presbyterian Church (U.S.A.)'s Task Force to Study Reparations delivered a series of recommendations in 2004 that were endorsed by the highest governing body, the General Assembly.[8] One result of this has been the adoption of a new confession by the church, the Belhar Confession, written by the black church in South Africa during apartheid. Perhaps the PC(USA) still should develop its own national confession about its complicity in racism in the United States.

How has your church benefited from racism? What would have to happen to initiate a conversation about this?

Did the land where your church sits originally belong to others, such as Native Americans or Mexicans? If so, what would racial justice look like?

A Different Approach to Mission

Many Christians have questioned some of the "mission" attempts by people with privilege and power toward groups that would not need help were it not for the injustice caused by the system giving those same missionaries their privilege and power. The relationships built often reinforce the power structure, as help is "given" without questioning the complicity of the giver in a system that produced the need. The shame felt by many churches aware of this dynamic has kept them from engaging in more prophetic, authentic mission, yet others have made justice the center of their mission efforts and used some of their privilege to confront injustice.

In 2002 some U.S. Christians became aware of lethal amounts of lead found in children living in the mining town of La Oroya, Peru. The mine was owned by the Doe Run–Peru Company, a subsidiary of the Renco Corporation of New York. Due to pressure from the United States on Peru's government to lower or eliminate environmental protections in order to do business, the pollution from the metal smelter in La Oroya made the town among the ten worst-polluted places on the planet, and more than 97 percent of its children under age six suffered from lead poisoning. Residents of the town, who needed the jobs, were threatened whenever they complained. Through a partnership with a network of Presbyterian churches and nongovernmental organizations in the United States and Peru called Joining Hands against Hunger, resources were leveraged to document the contamination, create and sustain a media campaign in Peru and the United States, and shame the U.S. company to quit offshoring pollution.[9]

Mission projects of U.S. churches often are inefficient, show an appalling lack of cultural awareness, have a negative effect on local Christian churches or social services, and focus on the personal transformation of U.S. members, often at the expense of local hosts. Yet powerful things can happen when relationships are built on confronting racial and economic injustice.

A number of U.S. churches are turning their mission focus to local efforts around racial justice. For example, some evangelical churches in Eureka, California, raised money to help the Wigot tribe purchase some of its nearby sacred land that had been stolen by the government in the twentieth century and eventually became a toxic dump, an all-too-frequent occurrence on Native American lands.[10] Actions such as this by white churches not only educate white members about racism, but they also give a strong witness to society and government that more must be done to right past wrongs.

The membership of Urban Hope Community Church in Birmingham, Alabama, is over 90 percent black, and more than 40 percent of its members live below the poverty level. Less than ten minutes away is the mostly white Oak Mountain Presbyterian Church, where 55.7 percent of area homeowners live in homes worth over $300,000. The two churches work together on social projects, including jobs programs and small business support. They have attempted to build relationships that include the white church giving resources but in a way that is not seen as rescuing the poorer church. The pastors, who organized a showing of the movie *Selma* for their congregations to watch and discuss together, say the relationship is not warm and fuzzy but is essential.[11]

Finally, members of Plymouth Congregational Church in Minneapolis are making long-term commitments toward communities of color in their city. After studying the book *The New Jim Crow: Mass Incarceration in the Age of Colorblindness* by Michelle Alexander, they hired a consultant to work with them for two years on white privilege and institutional racism. Their pastor, Reverend Theresa Voss, says it is important for a church to know itself before it can partner with non-white churches. The church has constructed a forty-unit housing complex for mentally ill and chemically dependent residents and is now working with other churches to build apartments for seventy-two ex-offenders.

Does your church participate in international mission hands-on projects? If so, who benefits?

Describe how mission projects in your community address racial justice.

Conclusion

In the midst of another period of increased discussion about race relations in the United States, many white churches and leaders have participated in protests against police killings and are making renewed efforts to build bridges with communities of color in their local context. Many other well-intentioned Christians are wondering what to do. Unfortunately, no blueprint exists. But we do know from a painful past that simply focusing on being nice to one another will not change the deep, systemic racism that is firmly rooted in the entire history of this country. If real change is to happen, it seems obvious that at least two things need to occur in order to take advantage of the moment. First, churches need to focus on doing racial justice and quit declaring some beloved community when justice has not yet been done. Second, a sincere confession needs to be made that includes fixing the wrongs done. That is huge and cannot happen by a single church or institution. But a movement can begin, and perhaps is underway, to work in this direction. Only movement over several generations can undo wrongs and repair damage. Churches, segregated or not, are well positioned to participate in the movement. We have the rich vocabulary and theology of confession, justice, and reconciliation running through the Bible and our tradition. Education is valued by our members. And our hope for God's realm where a beloved community will one day exist inspires us to continue working for justice despite the discomfort and confrontation that happens when we stand up for justice.

Racism was hard-wired into this country from its founding and then through its constitution and religious, social, economic, and political life. Undoing it will take more than reading a book or going to one protest. But change and transformation and hope are also in the DNA of the Christian disciple. Complacency is simply not an option.

NOTES

Foreword

1. Ta-Nehisi Coates, *Between the World and Me* (New York: Spiegel & Grau, 2015), 7.

2. W. E. B. DuBois, *The Souls of Black Folk* (Mineola, NY: Dover Publications, 1994), 2.

Introduction

1. In the summer of 2015, after nine years at the wonderful Second Presbyterian Church in St. Louis, I moved to Cincinnati to begin an interim pastorate at Mt. Washington Presbyterian Church.

Chapter 1: Defining Terms

1. Joseph Barndt and Charles Ruehle, "Understanding Institutional Racism: Systems That Oppress," in *America's Original Sin: A Study Guide on White Racism*, ed. Bob Hulteen and Jim Wallis (Washington, DC: Sojourners Resource Center, 1992), 12.

2. Ibid., 14.

3. Tim Jackins, *Working Together to End Racism: Healing from the Damage Caused by Racism* (Seattle: Rational Island Publishers, 2002).

4. Jackins, *Working Together to End Racism*, 1–3.

Chapter 3: 1492–1790

1. Howard Zinn, *A People's History of the United States*, 20th anniversary ed. (New York: HarperCollins, 1999), 8.

2. Quoted in ibid., 9.

3. John M. Martin, "Winston Churchill's Cold War: Kissinger Scholar Discusses New Book," Library of Congress Information Bulletin 62, no. 1, January 2003, https://www.loc.gov/loc/lcib/0301/churchill.html.

4. This method was developed by Robette A. Dias for Crossroads's antiracism training and organizing. Crossroads Antiracism Organizing and Training provides organizing, training, and consulting to educational, governmental, religious, and nonprofit institutions striving to dismantle racism.

5. Robette Ann Dias, "Historical Development of Institutional Racism: A Working Paper," revised May 2013, http://www.crossroadsantiracism.org/wp-content/themes/crossroads/PDFs/Crossroads%20Historical%20Development%20of%20Racism.pdf, 1.

6. Zinn, *People's History of the United States*, 2.

7. Quoted in ibid., 4.

8. Ibid., 12.

9. Sydney E. Ahlstrom, *A Religious History of the American People* (New Haven, CT: Yale University Press, 1972), 100.

10. Dias, "Historical Development of Institutional Racism," 28.

11. William Carl Placher, *Readings in the History of Christian Theology: From the Reformation to the Present*, vol. 2 (Philadelphia: Westminster Press, 1988), 107.

12. Zinn, *People's History of the United States*, 12.

13. Dias, "Historical Development of Institutional Racism," 28.

14. Zinn, *People's History of the United States*, 26.

15. Quoted in ibid., 30.

16. Quoted in Dias, "Historical Development of Institutional Racism," 8.

17. Quoted in Zinn, *People's History of the United States*, 31.

18. "Naturalization Act of 1970," Wikipedia, http://en.wikipedia
.org/wiki/Naturalization_Act_of_1790.

Chapter 4: 1790–1954

1. Frank H. Wu, *Yellow: Race in America beyond Black and White* (New York: Basic Books, 2002), 93.

2. Ibid., 94.

3. Quoted in ibid., 94.

4. R. Kent Rasmussen, Farewell to Jim Crow: The Rise and Fall of Segregation in America (New York: Facts on File, 1997), 2.

5. Quoted in Brown, Bury My Heart, 5.

6. Howard Zinn, *A People's History of the United States*, 20th anniversary ed. (New York: HarperCollins, 1999), 125.

7. Ronald Takaki, *Strangers from a Different Shore: A History of Asian Americans*, rev. ed. (Boston: Little, Brown & Co., 1998), 380–81.

8. Ibid., 382.

9. "U.S. to Pay Japanese Latin Americans Held during WWII," CNN.com, June 12, 1998, http://www.cnn.com/WORLD/americas/9806/12/japanese.reparations/.

10. Ronald Takaki, *A Different Mirror: A History of Multicultural America* (Boston: Little, Brown & Co., 1993), 173.

11. Quoted in ibid., 174.

12. Ibid., 176.

13. Quoted in ibid.

Chapter 5: 1954–1973

1. Tom Lewis, *Divided Highways* (New York: Viking Penguin, 1997), 193.

2. Ibid., 189.

3. David Roediger, *Working Toward Whiteness* (New York: Basic Books, 2005), 243.

4. Quoted in Kai Wright, *The African-American Experience: Black History and Culture through Speeches, Letters, Editorials, Poems, Songs, and Stories* (New York: Black Dog & Leventhal, 2009), 416.

5. Select Committee to Study Governmental Operations with Respect to Intelligence Activities, United States Senate, "Supplemental Detailed Staff Reports of Intelligence Activities and the Rights of

Americans," book III (Washington, DC: Government Printing Office, 1976), https://archive.org/details/finalreportofsel03unit.

6. "Willie Horton," Wikipedia, http://en.wikipedia.org/wiki /Willie_Horton.

7. "Independent Ads: The National Security Political Action Committee 'Willie Horton,'" Inside Politics, http://www.insidepolitics .org/ps111/independentads.html.

8. Taylor Marsh, "The Swiftboating of Harold Ford Jr.," *Huffington Post*, October 30, 2006, http://www.huffingtonpost.com/taylor -marsh/the-swiftboating-of-harol_b_32830.html.

9. Frank Wu, *Yellow: Race in America beyond Black and White* (New York: Basic Books, 2002), 63.

10. Helen Zia, *Asian American Dreams* (New York: Farrar, Straus, and Giroux, 2000), 205.

11. Wu, *Yellow*, 62.

Chapter 6: 1973–Present

1. "Ethnic Diversity in the Senate," United States Senate, http:// www.senate.gov/artandhistory/history/common/briefing/minority _senators.htm.

2. "Women in the Senate," United States Senate, http://www.senate .gov/artandhistory/history/common/briefing/women_senators.htm.

3. "State and County Quick Facts, USA," United States Census Bureau, http://quickfacts.census.gov/qfd/states/00000.html.

4. "The Voting Rights Act: A Resource Page," Brennan Center for Justice, August 4, 2015, http://www.brennancenter.org/analysis /voting-rights-act-resource-page.

5. Aviva Chomsky, *"They Take Our Jobs!" and 20 Other Myths about Immigration* (Boston: Beacon Press, 2007), 25.

6. "Restoring Voting Rights," Brennan Center for Justice at New York University School of Law, https://www.brennancenter.org/issues /restoring-voting-rights.

7. "National Update: Addressing Racial Bias in Crack vs. Powder Cocaine Sentencing," Partnership for Safety and Justice, September 28, 2007, http://www.safetyandjustice.org/node/1129.

8. "Criminal Disenfranchisement Laws across the United States, Brennan Center for Justice at New York University School of Law,

https://www.brennancenter.org/sites/default/files/publications/images/RTV%20Map.pdf.

9. *The Axis of Evil Comedy Tour*, DVD, directed by Michael Simon. (Chatsworth, CA: Image Entertainment, 2007).

10. Steven Salaita, *Anti-Arab Racism in the USA* (Ann Arbor, MI: Pluto Press, 2006), 41.

11. Ibid., 53.

12. "Hate Crime Reports Up in Wake of Terrorist Attacks," CNN .com, September 17, 2001, http://edition.cnn.com/2001/US/09/16/gen.hate.crimes/.

13. "Mass LA Muslim Arrests Condemned," BBC News, December 20, 2002, http://news.bbc.co.uk/2/hi/americas/2595391.stm.

14. Abdul Malik Mujahid, "In a Virtual Internment Camp: Muslim Americans Since 9/11," Sound Vision, July 2003, http://www.soundvision.com/info/muslims/internment.asp.

15. "Teens Hunt for, and Kill, Immigrant. Called It 'Beaner Hunting,'" Democracy Forums, November 12, 2008, http://www.democracyforums.com/showthread.php?p=326845.

16. Chomsky, *"They Take Our Jobs,"* 167.

17. The Editors, "The Real Sotomayor," *The Nation*, May 27, 2009, http://www.thenation.com/article/real-sotomayor/.

Chapter 7: Did Obama's Election End Racism?

1. David Jackson, "Poll: 29 Percent Still Think Christian Obama Is Muslim," Religion News Service, September 15, 2015, http://www.religionnews.com/2015/09/15/poll-20-percent-believe-barack-obama-was-born-outside-us.

2. Pat Garofalo, "Huge Racial Disparities Found in Lending Practices at TARP Banks," ThinkProgress, September 15, 2009, http://thinkprogress.org/economy/2009/09/15/172933/racial-disparities-tarp-banks.

3. Sarah Burd-Sharps and Rebecca Rasch, "Impact of the US Housing Crisis on the Racial Wealth Gap across Generations," Social Science Research Council, June 2015, https://www.aclu.org/files/field_document/discrimlend_final.pdf.

4. Zillow, Inc., "A House Divided: How Race Colors the Path to Homeownership," Executive Summary, June 2014, http://zillow.mediaroom.com/file.php/1759/Executive+Summary_FINAL.pdf.

5. Adam Liptak, "Supreme Court Invalidates Key Part of Voting Rights Act," *New York Times*, June 25, 2013, http://www.nytimes.com/2013/06/26/us/supreme-court-ruling.html?_r=0.

6. A. J. Vicens, "Native Americans Get Shot by Cops at an Astonishing Rate," *Mother Jones*, July 15, 2015, http://www.motherjones.com/politics/2015/07/native-americans-getting-shot-police.

7. See Gretchen Gavett, "Map: The U.S. Immigration Detention Boom," FRONTLINE, October 18, 2011, http://www.pbs.org/wgbh/pages/frontline/race-multicultural/lost-in-detention/map-the-u-s-immigration-detention-boom, and Ana Gonzalez-Barrera and Jens Manuel Krogstad, "U.S. Deportations of Immigrants Reach Record High in 2013," Pew Research Center, October 2, 2014, http://www.pewresearch.org/fact-tank/2014/10/02/u-s-deportations-of-immigrants-reach-record-high-in-2013.

8. Michelle Alexander, *The New Jim Crow: Mass Incarceration in the Age of Colorblindness*, rev. ed. (New York: New Press, 2012), 6.

9. Andrea Smith, "Heteropatriarchy and the Three Pillars of White Supremacy" in *The Color of Violence: The Incite! Anthology*, INCITE! Women of Color against Violence, ed. (Cambridge, MA: South End Press, 2006), 70–76.

10. Oliver Laughland, "New Jersey Muslims Seek New Ruling on NYPD Mass Surveillance Program," *Guardian*, January 13, 2015, http://www.theguardian.com/us-news/2015/jan/13/nypd-muslim-surveillance-court-plaintiffs.

11. Max Ehrenfreund, "The Biggest Question about Police Militarization Obama Hasn't Answered," *Washington Post*, May 21, 2015, http://www.washingtonpost.com/news/wonkblog/wp/2015/05/21/the-biggest-question-about-police-militarization-obama-hasnt-answered.

12. Paul Chappell, *The Cosmic Ocean: New Answers to Big Questions* (Weston, CT: Prospecta Press, 2015), 54.

13. Michael Martinez and Holly Yan, "Showdown: California Town Turns Away Buses of Detained Immigrants," CNN.com, July 3, 2014, http://www.cnn.com/2014/07/02/us/california-immigrant-transfers.

14. Scott Clement, "Millennials Are Just as Racist as Their Parents," *Washington Post*, June 23, 2015, http://www.washingtonpost.com/news/wonkblog/wp/2015/06/23/millennials-are-just-as-racist-as-their-parents.

Chapter 8: Do Segregated Churches Imply Racism?

1. Eric Michael, "The Most Segregated Hour Reformed African American Network, https://www.raanetwork.org/most-segregated-hour.

2. Thomas Jefferson, Notes on the State of Virginia [microform] (Richmond, VA: J. W. Randolph, 1853), 148–53, http://books.google.com/books?id=DTWttRSMtbYC&printsec=titlepageJefferson. The contention that Jefferson's book is a blueprint came from Smedley and Smedley, "Race as Biology Is Fiction."

3. James Henretta, "Richard Allen and African-American Identity," in *America's History*, 3rd ed., by James A. Henretta et al. (New York: Worth Publishers, 1997), http://www.earlyamerica.com/review/spring97/allen.html .

4. Gayraud S. Wilmore, *Black Religion and Black Radicalism*, 1st ed. (Garden City, NY: Doubleday, 1973).

5. Cheryl J. Sanders, *Saints in Exile: The Holiness-Pentecostal Experience in African American Religion and Culture* (New York: Oxford University Press, 1996), 19.

6. Ibid., 3–4.

7. Charles Reagan Wilson, "Religion and the US South," *Southern Spaces*, March 16, 2004, http://www.southernspaces.org/2004/overview-religion-and-us-south.

8. LeAna B. Gloor, "From the Melting Pot to the Tossed Salad Metaphor: Why Coercive Assimilation Lacks the Flavors Americans Crave," *Hohonu* 4, no. 1 (2006), http://hilo.hawaii.edu/academics/hohonu/documents/Vol04x06FromtheMeltingPot.pdf.

Chapter 9: Police Brutality

1. http://blacklivesmatter.com.

2. Liz Pleasant, "Black Lives Matter: Too Bad We Have to Say It, but It's Bringing People Together," *Yes!* (Summer 2015): 32–34.

3. Statistics vary because record keeping is sporadic, but one citizen database (http://killedbypolice.net) that contains links to relevant news reports put the number above eight hundred just between January and August of 2015.

4. Milton J. Valencia and Evan Allen, "Diversity in Ranks Limited; Mass. Police Try to Build Links," *Boston Globe*, September 2, 2014, http://www.bostonglobe.com/metro/2014/09/01/massachusetts-police-forces-lag-racial-diversity/RnEIJW5TuVki4ndotvl2GK/story.html.

5. Quoted in Jeanne Theoharis, *The Rebellious Life of Mrs. Rosa Parks* (Boston: Beacon Press, 2013), 197.

6. S. Danilina, "What Is Police Brutality?" *Black's Law Dictionary*, http://thelawdictionary.org/article/what-is-police-brutality.

7. Elahe Izadi, "Video Shows Seattle Cop Arresting Elderly Black Man Using Golf Club as Cane," *Washington Post*, January 29, 2015, http://www.washingtonpost.com/news/morning-mix/wp/2015/01/29/video-shows-seattle-police-officer-arresting-an-elderly-black-man-carrying-a-golf-club.

8. Joseph Goldstein, "Judge Rejects New York's Stop and Frisk Policy," *New York Times*, August 25, 2013, http://www.nytimes.com/interactive/2013/08/12/nyregion/10-years-of-stop-and-frisk.html?_r=0.

9. "Watch as One Boy Lays Out an Experience Most White People Will Never Have to Worry About," Upworthy, September 25, 2013, http://www.upworthy.com/watch-as-one-boy-lays-out-an-experience-most-white-people-will-never-have-to-worry-about.

10. Uri Friedman, "Do Police Body Cameras Actually Work?" *Atlantic*, December 3, 2014, http://www.theatlantic.com/international/archive/2014/12/do-police-body-cameras-work-ferguson/383323.

11. Greg Botelho, "Was a New York Police Officer's Chokehold on Eric Garner Necessary?" CNN.com, December 8, 2014, http://www.cnn.com/2014/12/04/us/eric-garner-chokehold-debate/index.html.

12. Isabel Wilkerson, "Mike Brown's Shooting and Jim Crow Lynchings Have Too Much in Common: It's Time for America to Own Up," *Guardian*, August 25, 2014, http://www.theguardian.com/commentisfree/2014/aug/25/mike-brown-shooting-jim-crow-lynchings-in-common.

13. Ibid.

14. Michelle Alexander, *The New Jim Crow: Mass Incarceration in the Age of Colorblindness* (New York: New Press, 2010), 100.

15. Alan Elsner, *Gates of Injustice: The Crisis in America's Prisons* (Upper Saddle River, NJ: Prentice Hall, 2004), 30.

16. Alexander, *New Jim Crow*, 105.

17. Shannon Sullivan, *Revealing Whiteness: The Unconscious Habits of Racial Privilege* (Bloomington: Indiana University Press, 2006), 40–42.

18. Eric Bradner, "Poll Finds Racial Divide over Wilson Charges," CNN.com, November 24, 2014, http://www.cnn.com/2014/11/24/politics /ferguson-wilson-cnn-poll.

19. Teresa Welsh, "Views You Can Use: Who Is Listening to Who in Ferguson?" *U.S. News and World Report*, August 18, 2014, http://www .usnews.com/opinion/articles/2014/08/18/race-impacts-perception -of-michael-brown-shooting-death-in-ferguson.

20. "Race and America's Social Networks," Public Religion Research Institute, August 28, 2014, http://publicreligion.org/research /2014/08/analysis-social-network/#.VenX2M5FWKw.

21. Julia Craven, Ryan J. Reilly, and Mariah Stewart, "The Ferguson Protests Worked," *Huffington Post*, August 5, 2015, http:// www.huffingtonpost.com/entry/ferguson-protests-municipal-court -reform_55a90e4be4b0c5f0322d0cf1.

22. Christopher Moraff, "When Cops Belong to the Community: And Enforcing the Law Isn't the Only Point," *Yes!* (Summer 2015), 35.

23. Ibid., 36.

24. Ibid.

25. Rahel Gebreyes, "LAPD Community Policing Strategy Serves as Prime Example for NYPD," *Huffington Post*, January 11, 2015, http://www.huffingtonpost.com/2015/01/10/lapd-nypd-community -policing-nypd_n_6446740.html.

Chapter 10: Whiteness and What White People Can Do

1. Jennifer Harvey, *Dear White Christians: For Those Still Longing for Racial Reconciliation* (Grand Rapids: Wm. B. Eerdmans Publishing Co., 2014), 51.

2. Ibid., 48.

3. Ibid., 50.

4. Ibid., 54.

5. From a transcript from *The Diane Rehm Show*, "Housing Discrimination, Racial Segregation and Poverty in America," which aired September 16, 2015, https://thedianerehmshow.org/shows/2015-09-16 /housing-discrimination-racial-segregation-and-poverty-in-america. The quotation is from Richard Rothstein, Economic Policy Institute research associate.

6. Ibid. The quotation is from Sherrilyn Ifill, president and director -counsel, NAACP Legal Defense and Educational Fund.

7. "Overview of 2015 National Urban League Equality Index," State of Black America, http://soba.iamempowered.com/national -equality-index/2015.

8. Thomas Shapiro, *The Hidden Cost of Being African American* (New York: Oxford University Press, 2004), 89.

9. "White People," YouTube video, posted by MTV, July 22, 2015, https://www.youtube.com/watch?v=_zjj1PmJcRM.

10. Quoted in David Remnick, "Blood at the Root" *New Yorker*, September 28, 2015, http://www.newyorker.com/magazine/2015/09/28 /blood-at-the-root.

11. Robette Ann Dias, "The Black-White Binary Obfuscates and Distorts: Why the Antiracism Movement Must Reject It," March 5, 2014, https://applyingtheanalysis.wordpress.com/2014/03/05/the-black -white-binary-obfuscates-and-distorts-why-the-antiracism-movement -must-reject-it.

12. Otis Moss III, "Hands Up, Black Lives, and Ferguson, Missouri," video at http://empoweringvoicesonline.com/rev-dr-otis-moss -iii-hands-black-lives-ferguson-missouri.

Chapter 11: The Church's Response

1. Otis Moss III, *Blue Note Preaching in a Post-Soul World: Finding Hope in an Age of Despair* (Louisville, KY: Westminster John Knox Press, 2015), 100–101.

2. "Black Manifesto," The Archives of the Episcopal Church, http://www.episcopalarchives.org/Afro-Anglican_history/exhibit/pdf /blackmanifesto.pdf.

3. "Sacred Conversation on Race," United Church of Christ, http://www.ucc.org/sacred-conversation.

4. "Seeing the Face of God in Each Other: The Antiracism Training Manual of the Episcopal Church," The Episcopal Church, http:// www.episcopalchurch.org/library/document/seeing-face-god-each -other-antiracism-training-manual-episcopal-church.

5. Resolution 2006-C011, "Support Legislation for Reparations for Slavery," The Archives of the Episcopal Church, http://

www.episcopalarchives.org/cgi-bin/acts/acts_resolution-complete
.pl?resolution=2006-C011.

6. Resolution 2006-A123, "Study Economic Benefits Derived from Slavery," The Archives of the Episcopal Church, http://www.episcopalarchives.org/cgi-bin/acts/acts_resolution-complete .pl?resolution=2006-A123.

7. See Jennifer Harvey, *Dear White Christians: For Those Still Longing for Racial Reconciliation* (Grand Rapids, MI: Eerdmans, 2014).

8. "Report of the Task Force on Reparations," Presbyterian Church (U.S.A.), https://www.pcusa.org/resource/report-task-force -reparations.

9. B. Hunter Farrell, "Form Short-term Mission to Global Discipleship: A Peruvian Case Study," *Missiology: An International Review* 41, no. 2 (2013): 163–78.

10. Harvey, *Dear White Christians*, 171.

11. Carmen K. Sisson, "Can Churches Lead on Racial Harmony?" *Christian Science Monitor*, August 1, 2015, http://www.csmonitor.com /USA/Society/2015/0801/Can-churches-lead-on-racial-harmony.

ABOUT THE CONTRIBUTORS

Mary Gene Boteler is the interim pastor at Mt. Washington Presbyterian Church in Cincinnati, Ohio. Before that, she was pastor of Second Presbyterian Church in St. Louis for nine years and was actively involved in the Ferguson protest movement with a remarkable group of interfaith clergy in the area.

Laura M. Cheifetz is Vice President of Church and Public Relations for the Presbyterian Publishing Corporation in Louisville, Kentucky. She contributed to *Streams Run Uphill: Conversations with Young Clergywomen of Color* and *Reflections Along the Way,* and she co-edited *Church on Purpose: Reinventing Discipleship, Community, and Justice.*

David Esterline is president and professor of cross-cultural theological education at Pittsburgh Theological Seminary. His teaching and research have focused for several years on ways to respond with courage and faith to the realities of racism and white privilege in the United States.

Jennifer Harvey is associate professor of religion at Drake University in Des Moines, Iowa. Her books include *Dear White Christians: For Those Still Longing for Racial Reconciliation*, *Whiteness and Morality: Pursuing Racial Justice through Reparations and Sovereignty*, and *Disrupting White Supremacy from Within*.

David Maxwell is acquisitions editor for Westminster John Knox Press in Louisville, Kentucky. Throughout his life he has been made aware of his white privilege through various experiences, such as attending the first racially integrated elementary school in Tulsa, Oklahoma, living with Latin American undocumented refugees in New York City, teaching in southern Chile, and living in a bicultural marriage.

Otis Moss III is senior pastor of Trinity United Church of Christ in Chicago. He is ordained in the Progressive National Baptist Convention and the United Church of Christ. His books include *Blue Note Preaching in a Post-Soul World: Finding Hope in an Age of Despair* and *Redemption in a Red Light District: Messages of Hope, Healing, and Empowerment*, and he contributed to *The Gospel Remix: How to Reach the Hip-Hop Generation*.

Debra J. Mumford is the Frank H. Caldwell Professor of Homiletics and associate academic dean at Louisville Presbyterian Theological Seminary in Louisville, Kentucky. A native of Kinston, North Carolina, she earned a PhD in homiletics and an MA in biblical languages from the Graduate Theological Union in Berkeley, California, and an MDiv from the American Baptist Seminary of the West, also in Berkeley. She also holds a BS in mechanical engineering from Howard University.

Jessica Vazquez Torres has worked for fifteen years in antiracism, antioppression, and cultural-competency workshop development and facilitation. She is an organizer and trainer with Crossroads Antiracism Organizing and Training and has been shaped by the Crossroads analysis. A 1.5-generation ESL queer Latina of Puerto Rican descent, she is active in peace and justice concerns, including worker justice, immigration reform, and antiracism. She is deeply committed to addressing social structures and cultural dynamics that marginalize and minoritize communities and limit their access to resources.

DeBorah Gilbert White is a diversity, inclusion, and social justice advocate. She is founder and coordinator of HerStory Ensemble, a community organization focused on the social and economic empowerment of women who are experiencing homelessness, who are formerly homeless, and who are at risk of homelessness.

Frank Yamada is the president and Cyrus McCormick Professor of Bible and Culture at McCormick Theological Seminary in Chicago. He is the first Asian American to serve as president of a Presbyterian Church (U.S.A.) seminary. Prior to becoming president, he was the director of the Center for Asian American Ministries and associate professor of Hebrew Bible at McCormick. He is the author of *Configurations of Rape in the Hebrew Bible: A Literary Analysis of Three Rape Narratives* and an editor for and contributor to *The Peoples' Companion to the Bible* and *The Peoples' Bible*, a cross-cultural study Bible.

CPSIA information can be obtained
at www.ICGtesting.com
Printed in the USA
FFOW04n0616110117
31205FF